a Visit to
Vanity Fair

a Visit to Vanity Fair

Moral Essays on the Present Age

ALAN JACOBS

Brazos Press
A Division of Baker Book House Co
Grand Rapids, Michigan 49516

© 2001 by Alan Jacobs

Published by Brazos Press
a division of Baker Book House Company
P.O. Box 6287, Grand Rapids, MI 49516-6287

Second printing, October 2001

Printed in the United States of America

Library of Congress Cataloging-in-Publication Data

Jacobs, Alan, 1958-
    A visit to Vanity fair : moral essays on the present age / Alan Jacobs.
        p.   cm.
    Includes bibliographical references.
    ISBN 1-58743-014-2 (cloth)
    1. Christianity and culture. I. Title.
    BR115.C8 J33   2001
    261—dc21   00-069762

Unless otherwise marked, all Scripture is taken from the King James Version of the Bible.

Scripture marked (NRSV) is taken from the New Revised Standard Version of the Bible, copyright 1989 by the Division of Christian Education of the National Council of the Churches of Christ in the USA. Used by permission.

For current information about all releases from Brazos Press, visit our web site:
http://www.brazospress.com

FOR WESLEY

We can only
do what it seems to us we were made for, look at
this world with a happy eye,
but from a sober perspective.

W. H. Auden

CONTENTS

PREFACE

EACH ESSAY IN THIS BOOK is a blend of cultural criticism and personal reflection, though most of them lean to one side rather than the other; in general the sequence alternates between the more critical and the more personal. I am deeply thankful to John Wilson of *Books and Culture*, Father Richard John Neuhaus, Jim Neuchterlein, and Matt Berke of *First Things*, and Jody Bottum of *The Weekly Standard* and, before that, also of *First Things*—the editors who first published most of these essays—for their indulgence and even encouragement of this eccentric mode of discourse.

A recurrent presence in these essays is my son Wesley, and to him, with all my love, I dedicate this book.

INTRODUCTION

I HAVE CALLED THESE PIECES "moral essays" because I can't think of a better name for them, and because I secretly like the term. It's an odd one, though, especially when used in self-description by someone who tries to be a Christian writer. After all, Christianity is obviously something far more than mere morality; and the word *essay*—meaning "trial" or "attempt"—suggests a degree of tentativeness inappropriate in one who adheres to a prophetic faith. To complicate matters further, some readers may object to the term on very different grounds: it sounds old-fashioned, and *moral* is a near relation to *moralistic,* a foul word to the modern ear. So the phrase *moral essays* requires some explanation, and the explanation requires some history.

In 1750 Samuel Johnson decided to commence a series of periodical essays on topics of his own choosing. They were to appear twice each week, and he decided (after much internal debate) to call the series *The Rambler.* Before starting this project, he composed a prayer—modeling it, as he often modeled his personal devotions, on the great collects of the *Book of Common Prayer*—and inscribed it in his notebook:

> Almighty God, the giver of all good things, without whose help all labour is ineffectual, and without whose grace all wisdom is folly: grant, I beseech Thee, that in this my undertaking thy Holy Spirit may not be withheld from me, but that I may promote thy glory, and the salvation of myself and others: grant this, O Lord, for the sake of thy son, JESUS CHRIST. Amen.

13

Perhaps this does not seem a particularly striking thing to do, especially if one reads the comments on this "undertaking" by Johnson's
great biographer, Boswell:

> In 1750 he came forth in the character for which he was eminently qualified,
> a majestick teacher of moral and religious wisdom. The vehicle which he chose
> was that of a periodical paper, which he knew had been, upon former occa-
> sions, employed with great success. The *Tatler*, *Spectator*, and *Guardian*, were
> the last of the kind published in England, which had stood the test of a long
> trial; and such an interval had now elapsed since their publication, as made
> him justly think that, to many of his readers, this form of instruction would,
> in some degree, have the advantage of novelty.

The problem is that Boswell has misunderstood the significance of
Johnson's project, for the early-eighteenth-century series of essays to
which he refers—especially the famous *Tatler* and *Spectator*, written by
Joseph Addison, Richard Steele, and others—were for the most part light
and fluffy things. They made humorous (indeed often satirical) commentary on the social habits of Londoners, but there was little "maje-
stick" about the essays, and the authors made few overt efforts to incul-
cate "moral and religious wisdom." This is especially true of the *Tatler*,
which, as Angus Ross has neatly said, strove to be "modest, friendly, dis-
engaged, fashionable, and self-deprecatory." The *Spectator* essays, Addison's in particular, were occasionally more explicitly moral in their
import. A devout man, Addison would sometimes append some of his
hymns (including the beautiful "The Spacious Firmament on High," still
sometimes sung even today) to his discourses. But he and his fellow con-
tributors to the *Spectator* understood the direct propagation of morality and Christian living to be beyond the scope of the humble periodical essay. In their gentle satire, these early series did no more than nudge
people toward reflection on their moral duties. The very idea that a mere
essay could "promote [God's] glory, and the salvation of [its author] and
others," would have struck most of their authors as impertinent, if not
arrogant.

It would seem, then, that Johnson conceived of *The Rambler* as an
unprecedentedly serious undertaking in the still-new genre of the peri-

odical essay; and indeed in its pages he regularly treated issues of the greatest philosophical import and ethical difficulty—a tendency for which he came under some criticism from people who expected from these biweekly discourses something more frivolous, or at least more lighthearted. As Boswell himself points out, "the grave and often solemn cast of thinking, which distinguished it from other periodical papers, made it, for some time, not generally liked. So slowly did this excellent work . . . gain upon the world at large, that even in the closing number the authour says, 'I have never been much a favourite of the publick.'"

But of course Johnson became increasingly favored by the "publick," and by the time Boswell wrote those words, *The Rambler,* collected in book form, had gone through twelve editions. Yet this landmark in the history of the essay would be little imitated: the didactic or pedagogical function of literature, which Johnson took for granted, would not survive the coming Romantic revolution, at least in any form he would have recognized. (It's not often enough remembered that that engenderer of Romanticism, Jean-Jacques Rousseau, was only three years younger than Johnson, and that William Blake's first book of poems appeared in Johnson's lifetime.) The great Romantic essayists William Hazlitt and Charles Lamb were brilliant, incisive, witty, and provocative but would not have felt comfortable in the teacher's robes that Johnson seems readily to have donned each day before his (habitually late) breakfast.

Another century and a half would pass before a worthy heir of Johnson would emerge—as it happened, two such heirs: C. S. Lewis and George Orwell. In one of the essays included here I say a bit about the striking parallels, especially stylistic, between these two writers, but at this point I want to focus on the trait that most closely links them with Johnson: their conviction that there is a common moral code that all human beings should, and almost all do, recognize. Lewis calls this the Tao and argues for its validity in several of his books. Orwell, conversely, never argues for it, but it is omnipresent in his work. In fact, Orwell's deep commitment to the Tao is the only component of his mind that enables us to account for something peculiar in his work:

sometimes even in a single Orwell essay we can find strenuous defenses
of democratic socialism combined with cold-blooded eviscerations of
the behavior and rhetoric of many English socialists. For Orwell, a particular course of action or political position is not right because it conforms to the principles of socialism; rather, socialism is right because
it conforms to this elemental and rock-solid code of morality. That the
strong oppress the weak is a fact; that the strong are *wrong* to oppress
the weak is, for Orwell, also a fact. If we want to call it a moral rather
than a historical or political fact, well, that is not particularly interesting to him.

(A necessary digression: It is not a belief in immutable codes of morality that characterizes what is often, and carelessly, called "Enlightenment rationality" or "Cartesianism" or "foundationalism." Almost all
Christians, long before and long after Descartes, have believed that
commandments to forgive one's enemies and to care for widows and
orphans and so on are binding on everyone regardless of cultural situation. What characterizes foundationalism is the belief that morality,
the Tao, can be argued for or defended in terms accessible and compelling to any rational person—that is, anyone whose intellectual equip-
ment is functioning properly. Neither Lewis nor Orwell shows himself
to be laboring in the Cartesian tradition simply by appealing to the Tao,
but Lewis's *arguments* for the Tao certainly derive from that tradition.
The essays in the present book follow Orwell's model, on this point anyway, rather than Lewis's. More on this later.)

Orwell had no party loyalty whatsoever; his devotion seems always
to have been reserved for the truth as he saw it, which is why he was
always in trouble with doctrinaire socialists. Once Victor Gollancz,
publisher of the Left Book Club, commissioned a book from Orwell but
was displeased by its critique of socialist practice. Gollancz couldn't
get out of the contract, so he printed the book with his own preface, a
crabby and outraged attempt to refute Orwell's arguments *before* readers could find out what they were. Such party-liners must dispense
with a trait that Orwell believed he possessed from an early age: "a
power of facing unpleasant facts." It is perhaps the most important
power that an essayist could hope to have; more than any other virtue,

it made Orwell, in V. S. Pritchett's famous phrase, "the conscience of his generation."

This exorbitant honesty and its concomitant disregard for the good of the party made Orwell even blunter and bolder in his moral writings than Lewis was. For Lewis *was* restrained by party loyalty—his party being the church of Jesus Christ. Some writers, A. N. Wilson prominent among them, have chastised Lewis for his "bullying" "police-court solicitor" manner, but if there is any truth in this charge, it applies primarily to Lewis as public debater. In his written work he is scrupulously modest in his claims; he strives, I think, to be winsomely irenic and as nonconfrontational as the rhetorical situation allows him to be. Even when he is dealing with thinkers whose ideas he believes to be utterly destructive—Gaius and Titius, for example, the school-master-authors who provide much grist for Lewis's mill in *The Abolition of Man*—he tries to give them whatever credit he can, even if it's just credit for not having consciously malicious purposes.[1] Lewis has to restrain himself in these matters, lest by excessive belligerence he cast the church itself, already in a precarious and deteriorating position in the English culture of the time, in an unpleasant light. Orwell didn't have to give a second, or even a first, thought to such matters.

This difference seems to me an important one. Lewis was right to take a kind of care that Orwell did not need to take. Christian writers, whether they like it or not, do not simply write for themselves; for good or ill, readers will see their work as reflecting Jesus Christ and his church. And if only for this reason—though there are other reasons—one must take great care when dealing with potentially controversial topics not to imagine one's every pronouncement preceded by "Thus saith the Lord." The law of love, on which "all the law and the prophets" depend (Matt. 22:40), mandates charity toward one's opponents in argument. Here too Orwell, though an atheist, is as salutary a model as Lewis; for instance, in the midst of a critique of the British ruling classes in which he has said that England "is a land of snobbery

---

1. For instance: "It is to their credit that Gaius and Titius . . . are better than their principles. They probably have some vague notion . . . that valour and good faith and courage could be sufficiently commended on what they would call 'rational' or 'biological' or 'modern' grounds, if it should ever become necessary."

and privilege, ruled largely by the old and the silly," he pauses to make this comment:

> One thing that has always shown that the English ruling classes are *morally* fairly sound, is that in time of war they are ready enough to get themselves killed. . . . This could not happen if these people were the cynical scoundrels that they are sometimes declared to be. . . . They are not wicked, or not altogether wicked; they are merely unteachable.

Except for the "unteachable" bit, this is just the sort of thing that people like Victor Gollancz condemned as giving aid and comfort to the class enemy. For Orwell it is mere honesty, and politically necessary honesty as well: "It is important not to misunderstand [the ruling classes'] motives, or one cannot predict their actions." Such a balanced view of things may well be politically shrewd. Certainly it is truthful, but it is also charitable. Charity and honesty generally go together, I find.

And charity and honesty so combined mandate humility about one's own conclusions—not timidity, or that vacuous failure of engagement that in our time passes for "tolerance," but rather a recognition that it is hard to know all the things one needs to know in order to make sound judgments about people and ideas. Therefore, it seems to me, the Christian who wants to engage in cultural criticism and reflection does well to take up the genre of the essay, with its intrinsically exploratory character, its reluctance to say the last word on anything. The inventor of the essay, Montaigne, put the point for all his descendants:

> This is a record of various and changeable occurrences, and of irresolute and, when it befalls, contradictory ideas: whether I am different myself, or whether I take hold of my subjects in different circumstances and aspects. So, all in all, I may indeed contradict myself now and then; but truth, as Demades said, I do not contradict. If my mind could gain a firm foothold, I would not make essays, I would make decisions; but it is always in apprenticeship and on trial.

But that doesn't mean that Montaigne lacked strong convictions or was reluctant to utter them. The motto he inscribed over the door of his study—"What do I know?" *(Que scay-je?)*—is often taken to be a rhetorical question, a verbal representation of the stereotypically Gallic shoulder-shrug; in fact it is anything but. He was passionately, cease-lessly interested in the extent and validity of his knowledge, and, in an age of global exploration, wrote in precisely that spirit. "What do I know?" properly understood is the motto of every essayist—along with another profound query posed by an elderly lady in conversation with the nov-elist E. M. Forster: "How do I know what I think until I see what I say?"

Let me affirm it again: charity, as can be seen from Orwell's treatment of the British ruling classes, does not require indiscriminate endorse-ment of people or ideas. I would not be practicing love toward God *or* my neighbor if I were to smile benignly on an unjust social order. It is not charitable to refrain from moral judgment: when Jesus says "Judge not, lest ye be judged," he is forbidding condemnation, not discernment. There are times indeed when Christian charity demands that one speak forcibly. I know of no better example of that than Johnson's great review of a rather too speculative theological treatise by a leisured gentleman named Soame Jenyns. Johnson tries to be forbearing with Jenyns, but when he gets to Jenyns's theory that the evils of this world are actually, though inexplicably, a form of good, his patience noticeably frays:

> He is of opinion, that there is some inconceivable benefit in pain, abstract-edly considered; that pain, however inflicted, or wherever felt, communicates some good to the general system of being, and, that every animal is, some way or other, the better for the pain of every other animal. This opinion he carries so far, as to suppose, that there passes some principle of union through all animal life, as attraction is communicated to all corporeal nature; and, that the evils suffered on this globe, may, by some inconceivable means con-tribute to the felicity of the inhabitants of the remotest planet.

> How the origin of evil is brought nearer to human conception, by any incon-ceivable means, I am not able to discover. . . . Where has this inquirer added to the little knowledge that we had before? He has told us of the benefits of evil, which no man feels, and relations between distant parts of the universe, which he cannot himself conceive. There was enough in this question inconceivable before, and we have little advantage from a new inconceivable solution.

Even here Johnson remains mindful of the need for charity and so continues: "I do not mean to reproach this author for not knowing what is equally hidden from learning and from ignorance. The shame is, to ... think, that there is any difference between him that gives no reason, and him that gives a reason, which, by his own confession, cannot be conceived."

But even Johnson's enormous capacity for restraint and generosity gives way when he must consider Jenyns's idea that our sufferings are possibly caused by higher beings who torment us for their sport. At this moment his patience fails—and rightly so:

> I cannot resist the temptation of contemplating this analogy, which, I think, he might have carried further, very much to the advantage of his argument. He might have shown, that these "hunters, whose game is man," have many sports analogous to our own. As we drown whelps and kittens, they amuse themselves, now and then, with sinking a ship, and stand round the fields of Blenheim, or the walls of Prague, as we encircle a cockpit. As we shoot a bird flying, they take a man in the midst of his business or pleasure, and knock him down with an apoplexy. Some of them, perhaps, are virtuosi, and delight in the operations of an asthma, as a human philosopher in the effects of the air-pump.

This displays the brilliance of a great mind agitated by righteous indignation; but does Johnson cross the line into mockery with the next passage?

> One sport the merry malice of these beings has found means of enjoying, to which we have nothing equal or similar. They now and then catch a mortal, proud of his parts, and flattered either by the submission of those who court his kindness, or the notice of those who suffer him to court theirs. A head, thus prepared for the reception of false opinions, and the projection of vain designs, they easily fill with idle notions, till, in time, they make their plaything an author; their first diversion commonly begins with an ode or an epistle, then rises, perhaps, to a political irony, and is, at last, brought to its height, by a treatise of philosophy. Then begins the poor animal to entangle himself in sophisms, and flounder in absurdity, to talk confidently of the scale of being, and to give solutions which [he] himself confesses impossible to be understood.

I think rather that this is just punishment for Jenyns's thoughtlessness. Johnson is clearly motivated here, as he always is, by great compassion for the suffering of his fellow humans (and for that matter, his own). Jenyns gives him ample cause for exasperation:

> Many of the books which now crowd the world, may be justly suspected to be written for the sake of some invisible order of beings, for surely they are of no use to any of the corporeal inhabitants of the world. . . . The only end of writing is to enable the readers better to enjoy life, or better to endure it; and how will either of those be put more in our power, by him who tells us, that we are puppets, of which some creature, not much wiser than ourselves, manages the wires!

Here, I believe, we see the moral essay (and in the guise of a humble book review!) at its exemplary best: striving for charity but passionate in its sympathy for human pain and weakness; aware of the powers of writing to help us enjoy or endure our lives, and agonized when those powers are neglected or abused. How unfortunate that many people think of "Dr. Johnson" (the title is part of the problem) as an Olympian figure casting down moral judgments from on high, for there has never been a writer more fully immersed in the quotidian pains and pleasures of this life, more constantly in the middle of human experience. Indeed—I hope it is not too reckless to say this—there is a christological principle at work in Johnson's moral thought, a kind of *kenosis:* he abandons the Olympian heights so often commanded, or striven for anyway, by the theologian and the philosopher and even in some cases (that of Francis Bacon, for instance) the essayist. One thinks of Kierkegaard's famously devastating comment about the Hegelian systematic philosopher trying to describe his own work:

> "If on the title page and in the announcements I call my production a persistent striving for the truth, alas! who will buy it or admire me? But if I call it the System, the Absolute System, everyone will surely want to buy the System"—if only the difficulty did not remain, that what the systematist sells is not the System.

> Let us proceed, but let us not try to deceive one another. I, Johannes Climacus, am a human being, neither more nor less; and I assume that anyone I may have the honor to engage in conversation with, is also a human being. If he presumes to be speculative philosophy in the abstract, pure speculative

thought, I must renounce the effort to speak with him; for in that case he instantly vanishes from my sight, and from the feeble sight of every mortal.

Only someone possessed of, or by, the essayistic spirit would have the perverse shrewdness to see the claims of systematic philosophy as a marketing scheme and the critique of System as a form of intellectual sales resistance.

Johnson and Kierkegaard are rarely seen as like-minded people, but in this passage I think we see that in one sense at least they certainly are of like mind. Kierkegaard's "Let us proceed, but let us not try to deceive one another" is an exact analogue to one of Johnson's most famous sayings. In response to some morally pious, but fatuous, comment by Boswell, Johnson pronounced, "My dear friend, clear your *mind* of cant.... You may *talk* in this manner; it is a mode of talking in Society; but don't *think* foolishly." The further, and more important, implication of this comment is that Boswell is justified in talking in that manner in "Society" but not with his friend, not with one whom he respects and with whom he hopes to have profitable relations.

Just a few pages earlier in *The Life of Samuel Johnson,* Boswell records a typically Johnsonian distinction: "When he once told me that he dined the day before at a friend's house, ... and I asked him if there was good conversation, he answered, 'No, Sir; we had *talk* enough, but no *conversation;* there was nothing *discussed.'*" In warning Boswell to clear his mind of cant, then, Johnson is also telling him not to insult his friends by merely talking with them when he should be engaged in serious conversation—which is precisely what Kierkegaard is saying to the "speculative philosopher" who fails to realize that claims to systematic finality are a kind of mere talk, a species of cant, that must be eradicated if we are to teach and learn from one another.

So Johnson, like Kierkegaard—though less self-consciously and paradoxically—speaks from among us, not above us. Yet he also continually reminds us that our ordinariness and finitude do not sanction moral indifference or the refusal to practice, publicly when necessary, moral discernment. The common moral vocabulary of our culture suggests only two possible stances: *ex cathedra* pronouncements or mute shrugs of the shoulder (thus our misinterpretation of Montaigne's motto). What is so wonderfully courageous about Johnson and his heirs is the determination to speak out on moral questions while refusing the temptations of the episcopal seat. After all, as Montaigne noted, "on the loftiest throne in the world"—or before the gleaming screen of the computer at which I type—"we are still sitting only on our own rump."

Well. Were Lloyd Bentsen, onetime candidate for vice president of the United States, to read these pages, he would doubtless remark, "I have read Samuel Johnson; I know Samuel Johnson; and sir, you are no Samuel Johnson." A just word! But Johnson and his successors exemplify for me what the moral essay can and should be. I suspect that in the right hands it can become the ideal vehicle for moral reflection in a postfoundationalist age; it can present or narrate or proclaim a compelling vision of the Tao without making the mistake of arguing for it. One of my hopes in publishing this collection is that someone with the "right hands" will read these scattered pieces and find in them a few tools appropriate to this great task.

1

A BIBLE FIT
FOR CHILDREN

IN A FAMOUS PASSAGE from *Science and the Modern World*, Alfred North
Whitehead gives this counsel to scholars in the various historical disciplines: "Do not chiefly direct your attention to those intellectual positions which [controversialists] feel it necessary explicitly to defend."
More important, and more telling for the deep understanding of a culture, are the "fundamental assumptions which adherents of all the vari-
ant systems within the epoch unconsciously presuppose. Such assumptions appear so obvious that people do not know what they are
assuming"—indeed they do not know *that* they are assuming anything—"because no other way of putting things has ever occurred to
them."

Similarly, in *The Discarded Image* C. S. Lewis notes the disturbingly
common phenomenon of coming across passages in old books that
seem perfectly transparent to understanding but in fact are hiding something. "We turn to the helps only when the hard passages are manifestly
hard. But there are treacherous passages which will not send us to the
notes. They look easy and aren't."

I think of these wise warnings when, as I often have cause to do, I ask
my students what Jesus meant when he said to the disciples, "Unless

25

you turn and become like children, you will never enter the kingdom of heaven" (Matt. 18:3). For everyone *knows* what these words mean. They are utterly transparent to almost all whom I ask; even people who tend to be shy in class readily respond. A cluster of concepts tends to gather around this saying like iron shavings around a magnet: children are innocent, I am told, they have simple faith, they have a sense of wonder. I have received the same set of responses when I have asked the question in church. And people are so easily confident in their responses that they are often surprised to note that Jesus himself employs none of these concepts.

Instead he speaks of children in terms of *humility;* but he employs this notion in a peculiar way. "Whoever humbles himself like this child, he is the greatest in the kingdom of heaven." That's the Revised Standard version of verse 4, but no translation erases the ambiguity: is Jesus saying that to enter heaven one must be as humble as the child whom Jesus presents to the disciples? Or is he saying that one must treat oneself as though one were no more than a mere child in order to enter heaven? The latter option, though no one I have ever talked to has come up with it unaided, seems more likely. After all, in most societies children do not have the full rights and privileges of adults; they are not free agents, they are under the authority of their elders.

One can readily see how accepting for oneself such a status would be congruent with Jesus' insistence that the first shall be last and the last first. And indeed many, if not most, biblical scholars have linked Jesus' statement to the low place children held in the culture of his time: people normally thought of children as unformed—or not fully formed—adults, who gained in personal value as they gained in ability and strength. (Consider the controversial claim made by Philippe Ariès in his *Centuries of Childhood* that "medieval art until about the twelfth century did not know childhood or did not attempt to portray it." In what Ariès calls a stylistically typical miniature, an artist attempting to depict Jesus' insistence that the little children come to him "has grouped around Jesus what are obviously eight men, without any of the characteristics of childhood; they have simply been depicted on a smaller scale." In this view, premodern culture lacked a sense of childhood as a state of human development with its own distinctive character, and that lack emerges iconographically.) But when I suggest to my students that Jesus may simply have been referring to the social inferiority of children, their enforced rather than natural lowliness, I am greeted with looks of perplexity or dismay or outright disapproval.

We might ask further whether humility is a notable feature in the children we have known. As sweet and gentle as my four-year-old son is, I would not immediately think of him as humble; for instance, he tends to be much more attentive to the shortcomings of others than to his own, and such a tendency hardly makes for humility. When people make their common assumptions about what Jesus meant when he exhorted us to become like children, they do not seem to be thinking about the actual behavior of actual children. Rather, an idealized picture of the Innocent Little One intrudes between their reflections and their experience. Lacking such an idealization, Augustine, in his *Confessions*, can observe the actions of infants and small children and see in them clear testimony to the doctrine of original sin:

> I wanted to express my desires to those who could satisfy them; but this was impossible, since my desires were inside me and those to whom I wished to express them were outside. . . . And so I used to jerk my limbs about and make various noises by way of indicating what I wanted. . . . And when people did not do what I wanted, either because I could not make myself understood or because what I wanted was bad for me, then I would become angry with my elders for not being subservient to me, and with responsible people for not acting as though they were my slaves; and I would avenge myself on them by bursting into tears. This, I have learned, is what babies are like, so far as I have been able to observe them.

This passage and others like it strike most modern readers as merely perverse, but it is not apparent that their views fit the observable evidence better than Augustine's.

I do not wish to overstress, after the manner of radical historicism, the differences between our world and that of the early church, as though a Hobbesian pessimism about children held utter sway then, and a Rousseauian optimism now. No culture is unanimous on this point or any other. Augustine himself, in one of his homilies on the Gospels, acknowledges that children can be humble, while some people in our time take a view not unlike that seen in the *Confessions*. Conversely, as late as the eighteenth century John Wesley, in a sermon on the education of children, could simply *assume* that every parent knew that children suffer from pride, willfulness, and a "natural propensity to seek happiness in gratifying the outward senses." But a serious transformation in our view of children has come about nonetheless.

Ariès contends that the belief in the innocence of childhood was almost unknown at the end of the sixteenth century but had become commonplace by the end of the seventeenth. *Commonplace* seems to me too strong a word, but then my knowledge comes chiefly from English culture, while almost all of Ariès's examples are French. It seems that the first time this note is fully and clearly sounded in English culture is the end of the seventeenth century, in the works of Thomas Traherne.

Traherne was an ecstatic and visionary writer whose works were not discovered until 1896, when a collector browsing through a London bookshop came across the notebook in which they had been scribbled. In verse and in prose Traherne celebrates the perfect innocence of childhood. "An antepast of Heaven sure!" he calls it in a poem titled, precisely, "Innocence"—"Within, without me, all was pure: I must become a child again." And in what came to be called *Centuries of Meditations*, one of the great prose works of his time, he loses himself in a rhythmical trance of remembered perceptions: "The corn was orient and immortal wheat, which never should be reaped, nor was ever sown. I thought it had stood from everlasting to everlasting.... The city seemed to stand in Eden, or be built in heaven.... Certainly Adam in Paradise had not more sweet and curious apprehensions of the world than I when I was a child."

If this sounds familiar, that is because it is an almost eerie prefiguration of the Romantic rhetoric of childhood. If we did not know that Traherne's work was lost until a century ago, we might suspect that Wordsworth (in his "Intimations" ode) was a mere plagiarist:

> Not in entire forgetfulness,
>   And not in utter nakedness,
> But trailing clouds of glory do we come
>   From God, who is our home:
> Heaven lies about us in our infancy!

Indeed it is only with the advent of Romanticism that the innocence of childhood assumes a talismanic status. In a historical world that always disappoints (especially in the disastrous and bloody aftermath of the French Revolution, for which hopes had been so high) the pull of nostalgia for an earlier and purer state becomes almost irresistible. In the terms favored by W. H. Auden, the Utopians of the eighteenth century become the Arcadians of the nineteenth; and while the Arcadia they long for can be historical, it is more often personal. "Carry me back, Master," Auden mockingly writes (and he is mocking himself, for he recognized Arcadianism as one of his strongest temptations), "carry me back to the days before my wife had put on weight, back to the years when beer was cheap and the rivers really froze in winter. . . . Give me my passage home, let me see that harbour once again just as it was before I learned the bad words." Ah, childhood! Perhaps when he wrote these words, Auden, a new resident of the United States, had already noted that Arcadianism is—even more than its near relative, Harold Bloom's beloved Gnosticism—the "American religion."

One early (and distinctly American) version or consequence of Romanticism was the Transcendentalism of New England; one of the key figures in that movement was A. Bronson Alcott, best known today as the father of Louisa May Alcott. Bronson Alcott participated to an almost Trahernian degree in the Romantic cult of the innocent child, which for him took a curious and interesting form. In 1835 he founded a school in Boston called the Temple School, and a key part of the weekly routine was a time for Alcott to gather his pupils together and discuss the Gospels. Alcott did not lecture but asked questions, trying to follow the Socratic example ("Plato for thought, Christ for action!" was one of his mottoes). He saw to it that these "conversations with children on the Gospels," as he called them, were recorded by a secretary; soon thereafter he had them published.

These "conversations" have been reissued under the title *How Like an Angel Came I Down,* a phrase taken, perhaps not surprisingly in light of the little history I have been recounting, from Thomas Traherne's poem "Wonder." The reissue came about because of the enthusiasm of Alice O. Howell ("therapist, author, teacher"), who provides an excitable introduction—"Oh, Boston, where is your innocence now!"—filled with statistics provided by the Children's Defense Fund, references to Carl Jung, and, yes, extended quotations from Wordsworth's "Intimations" ode. Also noteworthy are the facts that this reissue is published by the Lindisfarne Press, which is associated with the Anthroposophical Society, and that it features a foreword by poet and translator Stephen Mitchell, who has recently found it necessary to repeat the Jeffersonian project of producing an edition of the Gospels with everything that could offend a decent-minded liberal neatly excised. (The chief difference is that Mitchell had the resources of a publishing empire, HarperCollins, behind his work, while Jefferson had to make do with scissors and paste.) In such details the cultural history of the modern West is writ small.

The conversations themselves, though, are absolutely fascinating, because the children are fascinating. Here is a passage chosen at random:

MR. ALCOTT. What do you mean by Judgment Day?

ELLEN. The last day, the day when the world is to be destroyed.

MR. ALCOTT. When will that day come?

CHARLES. The day of Judgment is not any more at the end of the world than now. It is the Judgment of conscience every moment.

MR. ALCOTT. Ellen is thinking of burning worlds, open books, a Judge, an assembled universe.

LUCIA. I think the day of Judgment is when anyone dies; the conscience judges.

JOSEPH. Mr. Alcott, it does not mean any particular day; but they wanted to express how very certain and real the judgment is which goes on all the time, and so they expressed it in this way, for no words can exactly express it.

JOHN B. Whenever we do wrong it is a day of judgment to us.

MARTHA. Death is necessary for complete judgment.

EDWARD J. Death is necessary for any judgment.

AUGUSTINE. I do not think the world is to be destroyed.

All of these children were between seven and twelve years old, except for Edward J., who, despite his apparently Kafkaesque outlook on life, is listed as "under seven." Through the course of the book Charles emerges as one of the most interesting and resourceful, and it is not uncommon for him to establish a direction for the others to follow, as he does here. Charles seems in many ways a prototypical nineteenth-century Bostonian, capable at one point of insisting that the phrase "Father and Son" does not mean "God and Jesus" but rather "God and any man," and at another point of saying, "I think the mission of my soul is to sell oil."

But the most extraordinary child of all was the youngest, six-year-old Josiah Quincy, one of several Josiah Quincys in Bostonian history. (The previous Josiah, his father, had been mayor of Boston, as had his grandfather, who also served as the president of Harvard.) In the foreword Mitchell notices this, as I suppose every reader would, and quite properly singles out this amazing outburst from Josiah:

MR. ALCOTT. Can you say to yourself, I can remove this mountain?

JOSIAH. (*Burst out*) Yes, Mr. Alcott! I do not mean that with my body I can lift up a mountain—with my hand; but I can feel; and I know that my Conscience is greater than the mountain, for it can feel and do; and the mountain cannot. There is the mountain, there! It was made, and that is all. But my Conscience can grow. It is the same kind of Spirit as made the mountain be, in the first place. I do not know what it may be and do. The Body is a mountain, and the Spirit says, be moved, and it is moved into another place. Mr. Alcott, we think too much about Clay. We should think of Spirit. I think we should love Spirit, not Clay. I should think a mother now would love her baby's spirit; and suppose it should die, that is only the Spirit bursting away out of the Body. It is alive; it is perfectly happy; I really do not know why people mourn when their friends die. I should think it would be a matter of rejoicing. . . . I cannot see why people mourn for bodies.

MR. ALCOTT. Yes, Josiah; that is all true, and we are glad to hear it. Shall some one else now speak beside you?

JOSIAH. Oh, Mr. Alcott! Then I will stay in at recess and talk.

(Incidentally, Josiah stuttered, for which the recording secretary, Elizabeth Peabody, was thankful, because it enabled her to preserve Josiah's comments with greater accuracy than the speed of the children's responses would normally allow for.) Though the other children are apparently rather in awe of Josiah's ardent eloquence and enjoy listening to him talk, Alcott often has to remind him that it would be good for others to contribute. Once, when Josiah is expositing his theory that "temptation is always necessary to a real prayer" (!), Alcott gently asks, "Now will you let someone else speak?" But Josiah exclaims, "Oh, Mr. Alcott, I have not half done." All the same, the others do speak, though typically in single sentences, and occasionally they are overwhelmed by one of Josiah's extemporaneous cadenzas. At the end of one conversation Alcott asks, "Have all been interested today?"

MANY. Very much interested.

JOSIAH. I have been interested, because I have had a chance to talk so much.

MR. ALCOTT. Do you think some others were not interested, because they had no chance to talk?

JOSIAH. The next time I will not speak till recess.

It is tempting indeed to compile an anthology of the Collected Eruptions of Josiah Quincy—Emerson knew the child at roughly this time, and called him a "youthful prophet" who had "something wonderful and divine in him"—but I will confine myself to noting that the first discourse I quoted is very characteristic of Josiah (and in a different way of Alcott as well). For all of Josiah's verbal precocity, his inability to comprehend grief is an indelible mark of his youth. His remarkable conceptual sophis-tication is not, and perhaps could not be, accompanied by the empathy that we learn, if we learn it at all, from hard experience. George Steiner is almost certainly correct when he says that there are only three human pursuits that can produce true prodigies, because proficiency in them does not rely on such experience: music, mathematics, and chess.

Now, what are the concepts with which Josiah is so fully at home? Not surprisingly, they are Alcott's concepts. Alcott believed the Platonic doctrine of knowledge as recollection and therefore, as I have noted, prided himself on his Socratic reticence. He fully believed that he merely allowed the thoughts of his pupils to emerge; indeed when he became aware that he was directing, he censured himself and determined to pull back. (Today we would call him a "facilitator," God forgive us.) But he does make sure, here, to tell Josiah, "That is all true."

And it is interesting how fully Josiah has absorbed the gnostic ele-vation of the spirit and denigration of the body so common to Roman-ticism in all its manifestations. In a conversation about the nativity nar-rative, Josiah offers a characteristically extravagant and virtually Manichaean theory: that "the spirit comes from heaven, and takes up the naughtiness out of other people, which makes other people better. And these naughtinesses put together make a body for the child; but the spirit is the best part of it."

Alcott doesn't exactly disagree; he presses the children for their reactions to Josiah, and when they start to wander from that point, he (untypically) draws them back to it. Then he tells them what he thinks, which is that "God makes my spirit, and my soul all the time makes my body." This does not exactly make the body a compound of "naughtinesses," but it does place the body at one remove from God's creative activity, just as in the *Timaeus* Plato invents a demiurge to make the world so that the deity itself is not defiled by contact with matter.

Children, in the view I have been describing, seem to be more spir-itual than material: "Heaven lies about us in our infancy!" But they grow more fleshly and matter-bound as they get older. Alcott's students believe this about themselves.

Josiah. [at the end of one of his briefer discourses] You must be full of Spirit.

Mr. Alcott. Are any of you full?

Augustine. When I was a little baby I was full.

The Others. We all were.

Charles takes this belief to its logical culmination when, near the end
of one conversation, he pronounces this astonishing dictum: "God is
babyhood." (To which Alcott replies, "There is truth in that, I believe;
and yet it is language so liable to be misunderstood, that it had better
not be used.")

But now these children have lost that divine Spirit, which is the Spirit
of Innocence, and by repentance they try to get it back. It is not clear
that Alcott or his secretary, Elizabeth Peabody, believes that such a recla-
mation project can be successful. And I would be willing to bet that the
book's new editor, Alice O. Howell, does not so believe. For it appears
that she has no interest at all in what happened to these children when
they grew up. Howell tells us that one child, George Kuhn, died of consumption while a student at Harvard and that his sister Martha "grew
up to be a distinguished linguist." But not one word is spared for the
futures of the others, though the book has a formidable apparatus, with
forewords, introductions, notes, appendices, bibliographies, and so on.
It is as though the children cease to be interesting when they cease to
be children. "So that with much ado I was corrupted," writes Traherne,
"and made to learn the dirty devices of this world." In the end, writes
Wordsworth, the child comes to "Forget the glories he hath known, /
And that imperial palace whence he came." Little ones who have forgotten that palace and learned those "dirty devices" are no longer little ones; they have no more to teach us.

But who could fail to wonder what became of the marvelous Josiah
Quincy?

One may, perhaps, see signs of Josiah's inevitable fall in his comment about the "naughtinesses" that make bodies for us. How does a
six-year-old know of such things unless he has eaten from the Tree of

the Knowledge of Good and Evil? And once a child has done that, says
Ivan Karamazov to his brother Alyosha, he is one of us; he has defaulted
on our pity and deserves whatever suffering he gets. Ivan's heart breaks
only for those who have not "eaten the apple."

Josiah's theory about the origins of the body disturbed Peabody. She
thought it "very remarkable" but counseled Alcott to excise it from the
transcript of the conversations, or at least to remove it to an appendix.
He did the latter, but that theory, along with some other comments
made by the children in a discussion of Mary's labor and delivery—
which Alcott did his best to spiritualize—scandalized many Bostonian
readers, whose assumption was that Alcott had become a purveyor of
obscenity to children. After all, if children are pure and innocent beings
and have to be taught "dirty devices," then there is only one way to
account for Josiah's little theory: an adult has led him into wickedness.
The Temple School was out of business within a year of the publication
of the conversations.

It is not clear how one can evade such uncomfortable questions when
discussing religion with children, unless by eschewing all references
not only to wickedness but also to bodily existence. Yet how can Jews
and Christians preserve in their children ignorant bliss while teaching
them the Bible? For the Bible is full of bodies and wickedness. Would it
not be strange to say that some children pluck the forbidden fruit of
knowledge from the tree called Holy Writ? Yet every thoughtful Jewish
or Christian parent wonders about just this.

My son Wesley has two so-called children's Bibles. One he cares little for, perhaps because his burgeoning aesthetic sense rebels against
the unprofessional quality of the illustrations, which are by other children. The second he likes a lot, referring to it as "my Bible"—a locution
he doesn't use for any of his other books, which indicates that he has
picked up on the distinctive way that Christian adults talk about Bibles.
When he asks me to read his Bible to him, he always wants to begin with
the story of Noah and the ark, which is just fine, because the death of a
world of people and animals is not mentioned in this version. But after
Noah's rainbow appears, the mood of the text darkens rather considerably. Of course, the most gruesome tales are left out: we have no cray-

onishly colorful depictions of Jael nailing Sisera's head to the ground with a tent spike, or of Elisha unleashing two ornery she-bears on a pack of smart-mouthed punks.

Still, the list is a rather dismal one. Here's Isaac narrowly avoiding being slain on an altar by his father, followed soon thereafter by the various lies and deceptions of Jacob; here are Jacob's sons selling their brother Joseph into slavery; here are the plagues visited upon Egypt, culminating in the death of Pharaoh's young son. I find myself trying to skip forward to the less unpleasant parts, like the manna in the wilderness, or Samuel's anointing of David, or even David's slaying of Goliath. Unfortunately, Wesley is the sort of child who likes to go through a book from beginning—or at least from the point at which he chooses to start—to end, so we can end up wrestling ludicrously over control of the pages. How can such disturbing tales (I ask as I try to pry Wesley's little fingers loose from an account of Samson's massacre of the Philistine army) contribute to my child's moral and spiritual development?

The makers of such books have to deal with the same problems, as can clearly be seen in Ruth B. Bottigheimer's history *The Bible for Children*. Some decisions come, as it were, premade: no ceremonial law, no prophecy, no apostolic theology, no apocalyptic visions. Indeed, as Bottigheimer points out, what we call "children's Bibles" are retellings of selected *narrative* passages from Scripture, often accompanied by "commentary, verses, summaries, questions and answers, or bits of ancient history." But the question of *which* narrative passages to include can never be avoided. And if you think of children as pure and innocent—or even if you think of them as merely too immature or inexperienced to make proper sense of some things—you will want to exclude passages that might endanger their hearts.

But what Bottigheimer's history makes clear is that in earlier times people did not always think as we now do about what children can profitably read. Her project began when, while researching a book on the brothers Grimm, she came across a children's Bible put together by Jacob Grimm:

> I could hardly believe my eyes. Here, in a book for children, was Lot offering his virgin daughter to a rapacious mob, Abraham ready to slit Isaac's throat,

and Joseph sexually importuned by his master's wife. David committed adultery with Bathsheba, tried to palm her ensuing pregnancy off on her husband, and, when that failed, had him traitorously [*sic*] dispatched so that he could marry Bathsheba himself.

Later in the book, Bottigheimer shows that passages that no modern compiler would dream of including in a Bible for children—for fear of lawsuits, if for no other reason—were widely accepted in earlier centuries. For instance, Jael's pegging of Sisera's head to her floor "appeared in nearly every seventeenth-century German Bible for children, and the same held true in France." Most writers of that time heartily approved of her deed, though one English commentator (in a passage Bottigheimer does not appear to catch the inadvertent humor of) suggested that "though this act of Jael was of a most extraordinary nature, and God, for wise purposes, gave a sanction to it, yet we must not think of making it a precedent."

Increasingly, says Bottigheimer, the compilers of children's Bibles grew uncomfortable with Jael and began to surround her story with critical commentary (for instance, more than one gives her story the title "Jael's Treachery"); but the awkwardness of this eventually leads to the situation we now have, the exclusion of the story from compilations. Perhaps we do not think that children can appropriate whatever profitable lessons may be taken from this episode; perhaps we are not sure that *we* can appropriate them. Bottigheimer—whose research is almost always far superior to her interpretations of it—thinks that the story disappeared because society grew increasingly uncomfortable with the notion of a mere woman being the savior of Israel. But the status of women in Western society began to *improve* measurably at precisely the time the story of Jael started to fade from the compilations. A much more likely explanation derives from the cultural history we have been tracing here: a growing belief in the innocence of children leads to a growing determination to shield them from stories that might corrupt or wound that innocence.

Jael's case is an unusual one. Problems usually arise for the makers of children's Bibles not because they are uncertain how to interpret a story but rather because they do not know how bluntly they dare relate that story. No one questions the evil of David's adultery with Bathsheba; but how do you explain that adultery to children who may not yet know anything about human sexuality? Some writers, Bottigheimer shows, say that David "took another's wife," leaving the concept of "taking" ambiguous. Others (especially in the nineteenth century) make no reference whatsoever to the sexual nature of the sin: David committed "a shocking offense," one said, while another noted still more vaguely that "he grew tyrannical and began to sin." In my son's Bible David slays Goliath, becomes friends with Jonathan, and helps Jonathan's son Mephibosheth. Then he dies and Solomon takes over. Perhaps that's for the best. Maybe a four-year-old cannot quite grasp how David can be called "a man after God's own heart" and yet fall so terribly; nor, perhaps, can he comprehend the depths of David's repentance. But the essential shape of spiritual life is traced in the story of David and Bathsheba, and I wonder if it is ever too early for a child's mind to be directed along that path, to be trained in that shape.

So to the story of Jael I give a definite thumbs down, but to the story of David's crimes I give a fairly strong thumbs up. One could go through the list of potential inclusions casting one's vote, but if one is a Christian, sooner or later one must confront the most fundamental dilemma of all: how to depict the crucifixion. In Wesley's Bible it is the only act of violence pictorially represented. The nearest approximation is a picture of Samson wrestling with the lion, where it looks as if the two are playing. But at the end of the Gospel stories, on facing pages, we see Jesus reclining limply on the laid-out cross as a soldier prepares to drive a nail into his left palm, and then Jesus hanging on the upraised cross, the three nails clearly visible, his face showing sadness more than pain.

My cursory research, coupled with my reading of Bottigheimer, suggests that this is the modern norm. Few contemporary Bible versions for children avoid representing Jesus on the cross, though some tend to downplay the violence and brutality of the event: for instance, the illustration by the wonderful Tomie de Paola in his collection of Bible stories views the cross from behind. Older versions often were more sobering, not primarily because of their illustrations—none of those printed in Bottigheimer's book is Grünewaldian—but rather because of their sometimes hideously detailed texts. Modern Christians, it appears, don't think their young children need to know just how horrific death by crucifixion is, but they do not see how an acknowledgment and a representation of this particular crucifixion can be avoided. (Incidentally, Bronson Alcott's Temple School closed before he could get as far as the passion narratives.)

If children are going to be introduced to Christianity at all, we seem to think, the death of God's Son on the cross must be a part of that introduction. But perhaps the knowledge that at the center of our faith, at the center of our account of the world, lies such a death—perhaps this knowledge weighs too heavily upon a child. To paraphrase T. S. Eliot, after such knowledge, what innocence? And yet Christians, if we are to be Christians, have no other story to tell; when we stop telling of this death, even to our children, I fear that we are lost. What remains for us is what remains for Alyosha Karamazov. In a book that contains the most unsentimental, clear-eyed, and yet warmhearted portrayal of children in all of literature, he unflinchingly listens to his brother Ivan's cruelly detailed accounts of the sufferings of "the innocent ones"; he faithfully and comfortingly keeps his watch over the dying boy, little Ilusha; and at the end he gathers together "the boys" who have come to love him, so that he can proclaim to them the terrible and wonderful truth that alone can heal their grief: though there *must* be death, there *will* be resurrection. Absent such knowledge, what redemption?

As for Josiah Quincy, well, a quick trip to the library to consult the *Dictionary of American Biography* assuaged my curiosity. After taking bachelor's, master's, and law degrees from Harvard (where else?), he briefly pursued a legal practice before devoting himself full time to writing: poetry, fiction, reportage, essays. He married and had five children, the oldest of whom (named Josiah, to no one's surprise) became mayor of Boston. Our Josiah died in 1910 at the impressive age of eighty. The *Dictionary* tells me that he was "distinguished 'of mien and carriage,' democratic and friendly, and modest and unworldly to a rare degree." I for one am glad to hear it.

2

DOWSING
IN SCRIPTURE

FOLDED INTO THE CORNER of an old sofa, reading an equally comfortable nineteenth-century novel, I discovered an unoccupied corner of my mind with which to contemplate Wallace Stevens's great poem about reading. "The house was quiet and the world was calm." Indeed. But then it occurred to me that Stevens surely had no child in the house when he wrote that focused but tranquil line. *My* house was, according to the distressingly apt cliché, *too* quiet, and as I hauled myself up and lurched toward the bedroom, sliding in my socks on the oak floor as I rounded the corner with a Charlie Chaplin–style totter-hop, I had just a moment to wonder what my year-old son had destroyed and which of his preferred methods, dismemberment or ingestion, he had employed.

I found him sitting serenely in the middle of the bedroom with a Bible opened before him.

When he saw me, he gave me a white, pulpy smile, but as I stooped toward him, hand extended, he began twisting his head violently, after the fashion of cinematic demoniacs, to keep me from digging out his chaw. Eventually I retrieved it and saw that it was a small piece of the Bible, but the print had already dissolved, so I couldn't tell what part he had torn out. I looked at the Bible, but the pages I could see were whole and apparently undefiled. Of course I would have to find out; even in this most secular and unsuperstitious age, who can resist contemplating the prospect of a sign?

"Except ye see signs and wonders," said an exasperated Jesus, "ye will not believe." To put it mildly, it was not a habit of which he approved: "An evil and adulterous generation seeketh after a sign," he warned—which pronouncement, by the way, helps establish the doctrine of universal human depravity, because it is not possible to imagine a generation of human beings that *fails* to be evil and adulterous by that standard. Given the choice between, on the one hand, sign-seeking with even the faintest vapor of hope wafting before us and, on the other, settling down into certain knowledge that no sign will ever come, who among us would choose the latter? To Jesus' charge we can only plead guilty and quickly resume scanning the skies for whatever may be read in the patterns of birds' flights, in the odd shooting star, in the somber procession of constellations, or in the banners towed over football stadiums by droning little airplanes.

Or, perhaps, in the Bible. Does anyone still do as I once did: open Holy Writ at random, with uplifted chin and closed eyes, and solemnly drop a finger onto the page? No one ever taught me to do it, as best I can remember; it seemed natural and logical enough, as apparently it has to many over the centuries. When Christianity was still a creed to be eradicated in Rome, futures (including that of the emperor-to-be Hadrian) were read in the pages of the *Aeneid;* later, the *sortes Virgilianae* (Virgilian lots) were supplemented, quite predictably, by rituals involving a newly more authoritative tome. But the consultation of Virgil did not end: even in the sixteenth century Rabelais, in *Gargantua and Pantagruel,* has Panurge seeking the *Aeneid*'s help as he agonizes over whether or not to marry, and a century after that, not in fiction but in fact, the beleaguered King Charles I of England passes the time in an Oxford library by fortune-telling in Virgil. As it happened, Panurge and Pantagruel could not agree on what the lines from Virgil were advising, but Charles read in the Roman poet a foretelling of his downfall. At least from the perusal of Scripture one stands a chance of getting some straightforward good news, as Robinson Crusoe did:

> One Morning, being very sad, I open'd the Bible upon these Words, *I will never, never leave thee or forsake thee;* immediately it occur'd, That these Words were to me, Why else should they be directed in such a manner, just at the Moment when I was mourning over my Condition, as one forsaken of God and Man?

Encouraging though the random biblical word can sometimes be, this method of divination has not been universally endorsed in Christ's church. Edward Gibbon reports with characteristic wryness that "from the fourth to the fourteenth century, these *sortes sanctorum,* as they are styled, were repeatedly condemned by the decrees of councils and repeatedly practiced by kings, bishops, and saints." I might add, for the benefit of future historians, that they were also condemned, and with admirable and disarming wit, by a Sunday school teacher in a Baptist church in Birmingham, Alabama, circa 1972.

"A fellow wanted to know whether he should marry his girlfriend," Mr. Hutchins told his wretched flock of imprisoned teenagers, "so he decided to see what the Bible had to say. He opened a page and put his finger on a spot"—at this point I emerged from my usual stupor and sat up straight, never having suspected that anyone else did such a thing— "and it said, 'Judas went and hanged himself.' Well, he didn't like that too much, so he tried again. This time it said, 'Go thou and do likewise.'" A grin flickered. "So he tried one more time, closed his eyes, opened his Bible, put his finger on the page . . ." Mr. Hutchins paused for effect, with his own Bible open in his lap, his head uplifted and eyes screwed shut, his finger wavering presciently over the surface of the page. Then, suddenly, the finger plunged like a dowsing rod; he popped open his eyes and concluded: "And *this* time it said, 'What thou doest, do quickly!'"

Mr. Hutchins had confidence in the moral power of storytelling; he didn't say another word except to dismiss us. I repudiated my biblical dowsing—for several years, anyway. But I did wonder, as we traipsed off to the sanctuary for church, just what verse Mr. Hutchins's own finger had found as he told that story. Maybe his own destiny had been there for him to see, had he merely looked down.

O evil and adulterous generation!

Yet as Gibbon indicates, even the saints of the church have sought God's will in this way. Augustine responded to the child's call *(tolle, lege, tolle, lege)* by reading the first biblical passage that his eyes fell upon. Francis of Assisi and his companions, in the church of San Damiano, read three verses from the Gospels that became the foundation on which one of the great movements in the history of the Christian church was built. If these great saints were weak, then God made concessions to their weakness; and if he could do it for them, why not for me?

Why not indeed? But to anticipate such concession is fatiguing; for that reason, I suppose, most of us eventually tire of watching for our own portentous and unmisinterpretable sign, the one that will point our way through life and settle once and for all those nagging questions about where we are heading. About the time such weariness sets in, however, many of us have children and consequently shift our divinatory attentions toward their as yet unmarked lives. *Their* signs could still come. Thus my readiness to exercise all available hermeneutical energy upon the little tableau I had discovered in the bedroom.

But as I dug the sopping paper pulp out of my son's mouth, my mind occupied itself with a purely factual question: Who was that prophet who ate the scroll? A little later, when Wesley was napping, I got out my concordance and did some searching. Ah, yes: Ezekiel.

And when I looked, behold, an hand was sent unto me; and lo, a roll of a book was therein;

And [the Lord] spread it before me; and it was written within and without: and there was written therein lamentations, and mourning, and woe.

Moreover he said unto me, Son of man, eat that thou findest; eat this roll, and go speak unto the house of Israel.

So I opened my mouth, and he caused me to eat that roll.

And he said unto me, Son of man, cause thy belly to eat, and fill thy bowels with this roll that I give thee. Then did I eat it; and it was in my mouth as honey for sweetness.

Certainly an impressive performance, in its way; and yet the idea of Ezekiel as a role model for my little boy somehow failed to appeal. Part of it is the rather unpleasant aroma that tends to emanate from prophets generally; most of them don't like their work, and it shows. As Frederick Buechner once wrote, "no one ever invited a prophet home for dinner more than once." And Ezekiel is notably harsh even among those who share his job description. The Talmudic rabbis have surprisingly few words for him, and still less approval, perhaps because he presided, as it were, over one of Israel's greatest catastrophes, the destruction of Jerusalem and the ensuing Babylonian captivity.

No, I didn't even want to think about what bringing another Ezekiel into the world might mean, for him or for the world. The concordance directed me also to the New Testament—specifically to the book of Revelation, but this (as might be expected) was no better. The roll John eats also tastes sweeter than honey, but all the pleasure is in the eating; later it gives him indigestion. Moreover, John, who apparently wrote from a Roman prison colony on the island of Patmos, presents a prospect for Wesley's future no more appealing than Ezekiel's, though if tradition is to be believed he lived much longer than is common for prophets and apostles.

What does all this scroll-eating business mean, anyway? I thought as I thumbed through various religious reference books. Clearly it indicates something about the human encounter with the Word of God: these prophets loved its flavor, but at least one of them came to find it disquieting later on. Both experiences were familiar to me, though not always in that order.

Many years ago I heard on the radio an old-fashioned foot-stomping Bible teacher giving a talk on the importance of bringing the gospel to the unbelievers. At the end there were questions, and someone asked whether, because unbelievers by definition don't acknowledge the Bible as the Word of God, Christians should cite Scripture when seeking to convert them. The preacher had a ready answer: "Brothers and sisters, the Bible is the sword of the Spirit, so stick 'em with it anyway!" He was thinking of the apostle Paul's injunction to spiritual warriors to "put on the whole armor of God," including that sword "which is the word of God"; but he might also have remembered the unknown author of the letter to the Hebrews, who says that the word of God is "sharper than any twoedged sword, piercing even to the dividing asunder of soul and spirit, and of the joints and marrow, and is a discerner of the thoughts and intents of the heart." In other words, it's as dangerous to the one who wields it as to the one against whom it is wielded. Surely John had something of the kind in mind when he said that its original sweetness scarcely prepares the reader (or eater) for the pain that comes afterward.

Another warning from Jesus tells us, "Sufficient unto the day is the evil thereof"; there's no need to hunt for any extra. Is sign-hunting anything more than trouble-hunting? Clearly this whole *sortes sanctorum* business is problematic, and as I hinted earlier, over the years I seem to have lost interest in what it might tell me about my own future. Yet Wesley's little textual snack put me into a tizzy. However normal and natural it may be to shift our concern for the future from ourselves to our children, before Wesley's birth I had never suspected just how persistently speculative one could become about that future.

So I sat down with that chewed-upon Bible, plus a whole one to identify what was missing, and started thumbing through the pages. After a few minutes I came across a torn corner, and my pulse accelerated, but only until I saw what it was: the last chapter of Leviticus, with some commandments regarding how priests may set the value of certain unclean beasts that are brought before the Lord. I frowned, unable to find a connection. But then I realized that a very obvious fact had escaped me: book pages are printed on both sides. And on the other side was the first chapter of Numbers, in which Yahweh tells Moses to number all the eligible fighting men of Israel in preparation for the forthcoming war against the Canaanites.

I sat there for a few moments, thinking about war and history, thinking too about the character of Yahweh. But then Wesley woke from his nap. I walked slowly to his room and opened the door more quietly than necessary. He was standing in his crib and babbled smilingly at me when I entered. I picked him up and held his cheek against mine and thought, Sufficient unto the day is the evil thereof. O evil and adulterous generation.

3

PREACHERS
WITHOUT POETRY

MOST OF US ARE FAMILIAR with the story of the "two cultures," as C. P. Snow called it, or, in Isaiah Berlin's terms, "the divorce between the sciences and the humanities." When John Milton was born, in 1609, it was still possible to "know everything"—that is, to be competent in the whole range of available knowledge. But by the time Milton died, in 1674, the young Isaac Newton was already doing work in optics and physics so specialized and detailed that it would make such general competence impossible, and Europe's young scholars began to be confronted with a choice of intellectual paths—a choice that we still have to make today. By now that simple fork in the road of learning has led to the copious tangled bronchi of the modern university, a place in which even denizens of a particular department (biology, say) can speak so many languages that they are incomprehensible to one another.

Right though we have been to focus attention on this fragmentation of culture—with both its benefits and its costs—that attention has perhaps led us to neglect another extremely important "divorce," another bifurcation of a once-unified culture. I refer to the severing of literature and theology. Oddly enough, this parting of the ways occurred at the same time as the other one. The seventeenth century began with a series of figures—John Donne, George Herbert, Lancelot Andrewes—in whom literary excellence and theological acuity were equably blended. It was also an age in which certain communal projects yoking theology and literature that had begun in the previous century would find their culmination: the Authorized Version of the Bible in 1611, and the last major redaction of the *Book of Common Prayer* in 1660. In this period of English history—and one could adduce similar examples from elsewhere in Europe—the men of letters and the men of God were the same people, largely thanks to the Protestant Reformers' embrace of much of the learning retrieved by the Renaissance humanists. (In this development some of the second-generation reformers were more important than even Luther and Calvin: Philipp Melancthon's role in linking classical literary culture with Protestant theology has been much neglected.)

In such a context it is not surprising that the great models of prose style in the vernacular languages would be theological writings. From the sixteenth-century treatises of Calvin in French, Luther in German, and Thomas More in English all the way through to Milton's political pamphlets and Pascal's *Provincial Letters* (1656), theologians more than anyone else shaped European notions of stylistic excellence. This fact has not often enough been noted, but the blame for such neglect should not fall primarily on the secularization of the European intelligentsia. Rather, the chief culprit has been the Romantics' powerful redefinitions of *belles lettres*, which confined the literary to what they called "works of imagination"—imagination defined in such a way as to exclude almost all polemical or discursive or fact-based writings, thus leaving poetry, fiction, and drama alone to populate the world of what was now, increasingly, called "literature."

Strangely enough, it is the recent movement in university English departments from strictly "literary" study to "cultural" studies that has enabled a recovery of the literary significance of theological writings. The same movement has also led to a renaissance in the study of American literature, many of whose major writers (including Emerson, Thoreau, and almost everyone before the nineteenth century) have never fit into the Romantic literary categories. In light of these developments, it is not altogether surprising that the Library of America—a publishing program that, in its own self-description, is "dedicated to preserving America's best and most significant writing"—would now be moving toward fuller representation of certain "nonliterary" masterpieces of literature. Not that the library wasn't aware of such works from the beginning: its early publications included not only the work of Emerson and Thoreau but also the historical narratives of Francis Parkman and Henry Adams. But one senses a further expansion of range in some of its recent efforts: a two-volume collection called *Reporting Vietnam* and the book I am considering now, a fascinating and ambitious collection of *American Sermons*.

But however salutary this more expansive definition of literature may be in general, the claiming of these sermons as monuments of American literature is not a simple matter. Complex forces are at work here, and they require some investigation. Were these sermons to enter, or reenter, the canon of American literature, something would be gained; but a less definable something would be lost as well.

Michael Warner of Rutgers University has selected for the volume fifty-eight sermons by fifty-three different preachers. Warner is in some respects an ideal choice to do this job: a major figure in American Studies, he was also once, in a phrase he used in an autobiographical essay, a "teenage pentecostalist," and he graduated from Oral Roberts University. That was, needless to say, before he became what he now calls himself, a "queer atheist intellectual," and a founder of what has come to be called Queer Theory. But no hint of his current orientations can be found in his work on *American Sermons*, which is if anything too conservative, as befits a staid publication program like the Library of America.

Warner's selections can be analyzed and categorized in a number of ways that collectively tell a very familiar story about American religious history. Of the fifty-three preachers represented,

- 47 are white, and 6 black or of mixed race
- 51 are men, and 2 women
- 45 are Christian, 4 Unitarian, 3 Jewish, and 1 Mormon (Joseph Smith himself)

Of the forty-five Christians, only two are Roman Catholic, only one Methodist, and one Baptist. (I might also note that a famous painting of the English evangelist George Whitefield appears, inexplicably, on the cover.) For obvious historical reasons, Puritan Calvinists rule the denominational competition; for the same reasons, half of the preachers are New Englanders, including the first sixteen, though not any of those who lived in the twentieth century. The twentieth-century sermons included were preached by people born in South Carolina, Maryland, New Jersey (Hoboken), New York (New York City and Buffalo), Iowa, Florida, Missouri, Mississippi, Illinois, and Georgia—thus offering a nice illustration of the movement of American Christianity south and west, though not too far west. They also exemplify the proliferation of denominations, with their greatly varying theological and spiritual emphases. (Also represented among the modern preachers are Paul Tillich, born in Prussia; Rabbi Abraham Joshua Heschel, originally of Warsaw; and Rabbi Abba Hillel Silver, from Lithuania.)

One more classification scheme may be illuminating here. The sermons from the seventeenth century average seventeen pages each; those of the eighteenth century average twenty-two pages. In the nineteenth century the page count descends to twelve per sermon, and in the twentieth to a mere nine. (Some sermons in every period are reprinted only in part, but such excerpting is more common in the early ones.) This change may well indicate the constriction of the American attention span; it certainly reflects a change in the place of the sermon in American Christian life.

As Harry Stout has so capably demonstrated in *The New England Soul*, in Puritan New England the homily was central not only to the spiritual education of the already pious congregation but also to the communal life of the town or village. The Sunday morning sermon would typically last an hour or more—often much more—and would be followed by another in the afternoon, plus, in towns like Boston, a more scholarly "lecture" sermon would be given in midweek. By contrast, when contemporary Americans think of sermons, what first comes to mind is the evangelistic message—a homiletic genre that, following the enormously influential example of D. L. Moody, emphasizes brief exhortation rather than detailed exposition and is situated in a larger context of music and worship than the old Puritan congregational sermon was. Indeed, Moody always worked hand in hand with singer and hymnwriter Ira Sankey to create what would now be called a multimedia experience. The saving of souls was to be effected by a complex aesthetic experience of which the sermon was only a part—though in one sense the key part, in that it pressed upon the audience the need not just to experience but to actively respond. Still, one of the oddities of the modern world is that conservative Protestantism created and nourished an evangelistic enterprise in which the sermon was returned to a subordinate place in the worship service rather analogous to the subordinate place it held in sixteenth-century Anglican worship—just the tradition the fundamentalists' Puritan ancestors had determined to escape.

Let's look farther into this history. Warner points out (in a brief concluding "Note on the Sermon Form") that Puritan homiletic culture arose in direct opposition to standard Anglican practice in sixteenth-century England, which mandated only four sermons a year and suggested that they be read from the approved *Book of Homilies*, which accompanied the *Book of Common Prayer*. Seventy years later, the high-church archbishop of Canterbury William Laud would work to confine sermons to instruction in the catechism.

But between these periods matters were rather different. From the learned and intricate, yet sometimes brilliant, expository preaching of Lancelot Andrewes to the unabashedly flamboyant speculations of John Donne—whom T. S. Eliot, who came greatly to prefer Andrewes, would scornfully call "the Reverend Billy Sunday of his day, the flesh-creeper, the sorcerer of emotional orgy"—Jacobean England saw a great flowering of the homiletic art. In other words, preaching came to—or near— the forefront of Anglican worship, at least in London, just at the time that the dissenting or schismatic Puritans were leaving for America. Do we then see in these Pilgrims that same rhetorical flair and literary fire?

Not exactly. Warner is right to say, in an interview that the Library of America included with my review copy of the book, that American preaching's "best examples contain some of the most powerful lan-

guage we have produced." But it is important to note that the most carefully crafted and literate of the sermons that Warner has collected arise
from a tradition that explicitly rejected both the terrific erudition of
Andrewes and the poetic flights of Donne. Indeed, Warner inadvertently points this out when he quotes, in the "Note" already mentioned,
the guidelines for preachers articulated in William Perkins's definitive—
for Puritans, anyway—*Art of Prophecying* (1592). According to Perkins,
the preacher's task is to do four things:

1. To read the Text distinctly out of the Canonicall Scriptures.
2. To give the sense and understanding of it being read, by the Scripture itself.
3. To collect a few and profitable points of doctrine out of the naturall
   sense.
4. To apply (if he have the gift) the doctrines rightly collected, to the
   life and manners of men in a simple and plaine speech.

(This fourfold division could be simplified—as for example in
Warner's selection from John Cotton's "The Life of Faith"—into "Doctrine" and "Use.") The first three requirements would have placed intolerable constraints on Donne, who reveled in imitating the God he
believed to be "a metaphorical God," while the last would have thwarted
Andrewes's multilingual festival. Perkins's principles greatly restrict the
available linguistic resources of the Puritan preacher.

To be sure, Perkins's fourth point makes room for words of warning
or exhortation vividly expressed, but the anti-Anglican context of the
early Puritans seems to have prevented most of them from pursuing
these possibilities very far. It would be almost a hundred and fifty years
after Perkins before Jonathan Edwards would exercise this implicit freedom in the crafting of his most famous sermon—and one of the definitive productions of the first Great Awakening—"Sinners in the Hands
of an Angry God." (This is perhaps as good a time as any to note that
Edwards is, beyond any question, the most important American writer
not to have his own volume in the Library of America series.) In his
whole approach to preaching Edwards would come to emphasize the
importance of Perkins's fourth point: it was certainly necessary for

Scripture to be exegeted and exposited accurately, but as Edwards once said, "our people do not so much need to have their heads stored, as to have their hearts touched; and they stand in the greatest need of that sort of preaching that has the greatest tendency to do this." Though many would decry him and other pastoral participants in the Great Awakening for their indulgence of excessive emotions, Edwards remained faithful to this vision and would produce what may be the most brilliant and philosophically rich defense ever given of the proper role of emotion in the moral and spiritual life, the *Treatise Concerning Religious Affections* of 1746.

Nevertheless, as is well known, Edwards eschewed the usual tricks and resources of the orator in delivering even so explosive a sermon as "Sinners in the Hands of an Angry God." As a witness recorded, Edwards spoke in a quiet, level, even monotonous voice and made almost no gestures and he rarely lifted his head to look at his congregation; nevertheless, "there was such a breathing of distress, and weeping, that the preacher was obliged to speak to the people and desire silence, that he might be heard." Consider: while philosophers have traditionally linked literature and rhetoric as sister arts that lack the intellectual rigor and explicit foundations of the dialectic, Edwards would exploit every possible literary device yet scorn his era's ideals of eloquence. It is possible, of course, to argue that Edwards was actually being very attentive to the rhetorical dimensions of his preaching by speaking such wild and violent words in a quiet and monotonous voice, but the eyewitnesses seem not to have thought that he was striving for effect. If we do not recognize this distinction we deprive ourselves of valuable terms with which to evaluate speakers—or else we have to replace the terms we have forgone with others. To paraphrase Orwell, all speeches may be rhetorical, but some are more rhetorical than others.

As is also well known, Edwards's successors, especially among the evangelists of the last century and a half, have not shared his restraint; indeed, they considered the kind of response Edwards elicited as the pearl of great price that they would spare no effort or machination to achieve. We are only partly right to deplore this tendency. It is necessary to remember that Edwards was preaching to a congregation that was by our standards remarkably learned in Christian theology: they had been listening to sermons like his for some time ("Sinners in the Hands of an Angry God" was part of the "application" phase of Perkins's scheme and had been prepared for by more strictly expository preaching). D. L. Moody, Billy Sunday, and Billy Graham could count on no such preparatory knowledge and were therefore limited in the kinds of sermons they *could* preach. If we think their sermons are overly emotional and lack significant content, then we must see the flaw as located not necessarily in them but in the whole enterprise of the evangelistic crusade, which by its very nature demands a simple emotional appeal. And yet in an increasingly multiethnic America, the evangelistic crusade has done for the Christian faith what no other cultural institution, as far as I can see, could possibly have done. People who become Christians for what some would term "the wrong reasons" can be tutored and developed in the faith; people who do not become Christians at all, obviously, cannot.

But would we want to say that as the American sermon becomes less expository and more hortatory—addressed more toward the heart and the will than to the understanding—it becomes more literary? It is certainly tempting to say so, for our most common definitions of literature link it to the heart rather than to the head. But if Edwards could produce, or attempt to produce, sermons that were literary but not rhetorical, it might also be possible to preach sermons that are rhetorical but not literary. It is worth noting in this context that the earlier sermons in this collection were in every case crafted as *written* words; only after the composition was complete did the preachers memorize and recite, rather than simply read, their homilies. (In this practice they were following ancient models of rhetoric, which divided the art of speaking into five parts: *inventio*, or the generation of ideas; *dispositio*, or the organization of those ideas; *elocutio*, or the putting of those ideas into a suitable style; *memoria*, or memorization; and *pronuntiatio*, or delivery. It is not clear, by the way, that Edwards followed either the fourth or the fifth step, in that he read from a printed text and paid no attention to vocal performance.) Thus the sermon in this tradition is, in at least one of the strongest senses of the word, a literary enterprise.

By contrast, many of the nineteenth- and twentieth-century sermons reprinted here were never written down but rather were recorded and transcribed by listeners. Though such sermons may well have been carefully crafted in the preacher's mind, they sometimes depended on inspirations of the moment, and they certainly relied heavily on the art of *pronuntiatio*. A sermon by one Brother Carper, here called "The Shadow of a Great Rock in a Weary Land," was preached (probably in the 1840s) in the hearing of a Methodist missionary in Missouri named James V. Watson. Watson was much taken with the sermon and with the preacher—the son of a slave woman and her master—who in Watson's opinion preached with "the genius of an Apollos and the force of an Apostle." Watson recorded that Brother Carper "read with hesitancy and inaccuracy; seeming to depend less upon the text to guide him, than his memory," but when Brother Carper got going, his delivery was clearly so vital to his success that Watson made a point of recording his speech phonetically:

> But, brederen, de joy ob de belieber in Jesus am set forth in a figerative man-
> ner in the text [Isaiah 32:2]. It am compared to water to dem what be dying
> ob thirst. O, how sweet to de taste ob de desert traveler sweltering under a
> burning sun, as if creation was a great furnace! Water, sweet, sparklin', livin',
> bubblin', silvery water, how does his languid eye brighten as he suddenly sees
> it gushing up at his feet like milk from de fountain ob lub, or leaping from de
> sides ob de mountain rock like a relief angel from heben. He drinks long and
> gratefully, and feels again de blessed pulsations ob being.

However imperfectly, Watson's transcription captures some of the energy that must have driven Brother Carper: balanced clauses estab-lish a rhythm, while a curious and not wholly describable beauty arises from the combination of colloquial grammar ("it am compared") with a highly "literary" vocabulary ("silvery," "languid," "pulsations"). Still, as one reads Watson's account, one is aware of a certain lack of access to an experience that seems to have transfixed its audience.

But another black preacher in this collection benefits exceedingly by the art of transcription, perhaps because he was blessed with a more artful transcriber. Zora Neale Hurston—one of his century's major

American writers—records for us a sermon delivered in Eau Gallie,
Florida, by C. C. Lovelace, about whom, apparently, nothing is known.
Hurston represents the preacher's brilliant poetic flights by changing
the format from prose to verse when he really sets sail:

> And one of de disciples called Jesus
> "Master!! Carest thou not that we perish?"
> And He arose
> And de storm was in its pitch
> And de lightnin played on His raiments as He stood on the prow of the boat
> And placed His foot upon the neck of the storm
> And spoke to the howlin winds
> And de sea fell at his feet like a marble floor
> And de thunders went back in their vault
> Then He set down on de rim of de ship
> And took the hooks of His power
> And lifted de billows in His lap
> And rocked de winds to sleep on His arm
> And said "Peace be still."

"The preacher is a true poet," Hurston later wrote, and this poem is not
one I am likely to forget.

With the exception of Sister Aimee Semple McPherson—whose vivid
sermon gives every appearance of having been transcribed from speech,
using as it does a dialogue format that would be fully comprehensible
only if it were spoken—the white evangelists don't come off as well.
Least impressive of all is Joseph Smith, the founder of the Mormon faith,
whose sermon is a farrago of incoherent statements, leavened by a kind
of swaggering defensiveness: "I have now preached a little Latin, a little Hebrew, Greek, and German; and I have fulfilled all. I am not so big
a fool as many have taken me to be. The Germans know that I read the
German correctly." (This accompanied by repeated claims to moral
perfection: "I never think any evil, nor do anything to the harm of my
fellow-man.") But the Christian evangelists fare only somewhat better,
and that's largely because they lack Smith's egregious character flaws.

Perhaps it is because preaching of their kind is familiar to me from my
childhood; or perhaps it is because the virtues of their particular rhetor-

ical styles do not survive transcription; or perhaps it is because the larger musical and, yes, liturgical context of the crusade is missing; but the sermons of D. L. Moody and R. A. Torrey seem to lack all fire and verve.

> You ask me to explain regeneration. I can not do it. But one thing I know—that I have been regenerated. All the infidels and skeptics could not make me feel differently. I feel a different man than I did twenty-one years ago last March, when God gave me a new heart. I have not sworn since that night, and I have no desire to swear. I delight to labor for God, and all the influences of the world can not convince me that I am not a different man.

Three hundred years before Moody uttered these words, William Perkins was counseling preachers to employ the plain style and shun ostentation. But Moody's style seems *so* plain, so utterly unadorned, as to be altogether without character. The rhythms are simplistic, the vocabulary limited and colorless; the whole text shuns vivid image or metaphor. Yet Moody was undoubtedly an immensely effective evangelist. Whatever virtues he possessed simply do not appear in this context, while the verbal power of C. C. Lovelace fairly blows out of the page, like a holy version of the storm Jesus stilled.

And that raises a question about the governing notion of Warner's collection, that the sermon is a kind of literature. It would seem, to judge by this exemplary collection, that American preaching is rarely very literary: seldom does it exhibit the kind of linguistic inventiveness we associate with great writing. At the beginning of its history it is unliterary on (anti-Anglican) principle, though preachers could have exhibited more literary style; later it is unliterary because the preachers have few or no literary resources and because it becomes more strictly oratorical. Among all the preachers represented here, only Edwards and the black preachers combine theological depth and the mastery of language. And only in Edwards's case is that mastery strictly literary. Therefore, the interest of Warner's book, while great indeed, is primarily theological and historical rather than aesthetic.

Some would protest at the distinctions I have made—between rhetorical and nonrhetorical preaching, between literature and rhetoric, between theological-historical interest and aesthetic interest, and

so on. I have said that we may thank the movement of literary scholars toward cultural studies for Warner's collection, and that is true, but
certainly the current arbiters of cultural studies would strenuously
deny the distinction between literary and nonliterary texts. Stephen
Greenblatt, the founder of the movement called New Historicism,
wrote some years ago that "literary and non-literary texts circulate
inseparably" in a culture, which is undoubtedly true; but that very
point, as Greenblatt understood when he made it, relies on our ability to distinguish between those two types of texts. Greenblatt's successors, in their pious and, they believe, radically historicizing urge
not to privilege the literary, refuse so to discriminate; but they are
wrong to refuse.

It would be enough to say that they are wrong because distinction,
discrimination, is near the heart of any intellectual enterprise. As the
philosopher Bernard Williams has noted in a different context, we are
often in our thinking unnecessarily reductive and end by suffering
from a kind of poverty of concepts: we don't account for different phe-
nomena very well because we don't have enough distinct terms with
which to talk about them. But in the case at hand, historical reasons
for preserving the distinction between the literary and nonliterary are
still more compelling. The most literate of American preachers formed
their homiletical practice in contrast to a group of preachers they
found overly literary (though that is not the word they would have
used). For them, the realm of beautiful language was a seductive and
spiritually dangerous one, thus Perkins's insistence on a plain style
of exposition. Literary embellishment is a form of vanity, both in the
usual sense and in the sense employed by Ecclesiastes: "Saith the
Preacher, vanity of vanities; all is vanity." The divorce between literature and theology that I lamented in my opening paragraphs never
happened in America because the two were never married in the first
place—indeed they were barely acquainted, and their relationship
was characterized by mistrust, especially on the theological side.

Michael Warner's mistrust of the philosophical validity of this distinction between the literary and the nonliterary has, then, a curious
result. In the book he has edited, we find the history of the American ser-

mon wonderfully encapsulated—and much of the salient history of American religion encapsulated along with it. But the impetus for this collection was a literary enterprise, a context into which these sermons manifestly do not fit. A truly literary anthology of American sermons would look very different from this one; but I doubt it would be nearly as good.

4

AN EXCHANGE
OF FEARS

As a child I had no fear of death, but the very thought of eternity made the pit of my stomach lurch and plunge. Though the phrase "eternal life" is apparently full of comfort for others, it frightened me because I couldn't get my mind around it, couldn't conceive of endless duration—which is of course what I thought eternity was. When, a few years ago, I told a friend about this fear, he laughed and called me the Little Existentialist; he pictured me as a toddler wearing a cocked beret, a cigarette drooping from the corner of my mouth. I was not amused. Or not much.

The scariest picture in our illustrated family Bible was, I thought, the picture of the millennium, in which the lion lay down with the lamb and the little children frolicked—well, nothing so energetic as "frolicked," maybe "loafed"—in their white robes. I could scarcely bring myself to look at it, and yet I was drawn to it and meditated on it almost daily. I knew nothing of the millennium yet and thus was unaware that the pictured state of affairs (according to the interpretive tradition in which I would be educated) will last only a thousand years before being replaced by something utterly unimaginable in its glory, or at least unpicturable. The illustration was, to me, eternity itself. There were no scenes depicting eternal punishment in our Bible—though I seem to recall a picture of the lake of eternal fire into which Satan will at the end of time be thrown, along with all his followers. In my memory the surface of the lake is undisturbed, but even if scalded bodies had been depicted thrashing about in the flames I don't think they would have held the same terror for me as the lion-lamb-and-children painting, in part because, like most people, I have never expected to go to hell, but also because I find eternal punishment more comprehensible than eternal bliss. When I saw Doré's illustrations of Dante's *Inferno*—I was no more than ten, but already a veteran of *Ewigkeitangst*—my chief reaction was a merely clinical curiosity: I wondered if Doré's pictures accurately represented what a severed head or the uncauterized, unhealed stump of a leg would look like. And if so (a more sinister question), how did he know? Whatever the answers, these engravings never prompted me to consider my own future state.

Similarly, the picture, in that same family Bible, of an elderly John the Evangelist sitting at his desk and envisioning, in a kind of soft-focus bubble floating above him, the golden streets of the New Jerusalem, struck me as merely insipid. If the New Jerusalem is no more than a gold-lamé Manhattan, I thought, who needs it? (Later, when I was told that the island of Patmos, where John says he received his revelation, was a Roman prison colony, I wondered how, then, he had gotten such a handsome desk and such elegant flowing robes.)

Only one other religious image from my childhood had an effect on me even remotely comparable to that of the millennial painting in our Bible. Once when I was in my dentist's waiting room (I don't remember how old I was, probably no more than twelve) I found buried in a stack of magazines a small evangelistic tract, illustrated in comic-book style. It described the fate of a soul after death and showed people standing in a great line before the distant throne of God. When one of them, the protagonist of this cautionary tale, got to the head of the line, he was made to watch, projected before him on some otherworldly screen, a kind of movie of his life. He writhed in an agony of guilt as his sins were played out before him. Short, sharp lines radiated from his head, these, I knew from long experience with the highly conventionalized iconography of comic books, represented surprise. For some reason that I still don't understand, the *cinematic* nature of the ordeal was what jarred me, not the confrontation with one's sins as such. Though I probably already had heard—thanks to infrequent visits to Sunday school and my annual summer fortnight in Vacation Bible School—Jesus' warning that we will give an account of every idle word at the day of judgment, the admonition had never made any real impact on me. But that empyrean theater, coupled with that halo of shocked surprise, gave me a jolt. Still, even such a triumph of proselytizing suasion could not match in its effect that strange picture of the white-robed children petting lions and exchanging smiles with all manner of rough beasts. That was eternity, O fearful eternity, for me.

Eternity doesn't frighten me anymore, in part because I now know better than to try to imagine endless duration. Eternity is a timeless state, not a perpetual continuation of ordinary time, or so I have come to believe. (According to Hannah Arendt in *The Human Condition*, what I was trying unsuccessfully to imagine is immortality, "endurance in time," not eternity, eternity being the state of having no beginning as well as no ending. In that sense, of course, none of us is eternal. But if the afterlife is in some sense outside of time and not an interminable continuation of chronology, then *immortality* isn't the precise word either. I am therefore, with reference to Arendt's categories, in a kind of terminological limbo.) Now, I can't imagine living atemporally either—just the opposite: the notion is *so* utterly incomprehensible, so foreign to any human experience, that it lacks the power to frighten. The concept of endless duration, by contrast, is capable of generating fear because it is a drastic extension of something quite familiar.

But the more important reason that eternity doesn't frighten me is that I'm too busy fearing death—that is, I fear ceasing to be. Why worry about eternity if there are more pressing, more potentially immediate, concerns? And yet this fear of death, though it sometimes wakes me in the night with cold sweats and wild dread, is something I do not wish to lose—at least not by ordinary means.

The "ordinary means" I refer to are the variations on Stoicism that seem to mark the usual responses to this problem. I have become quite familiar with these responses, not through any intentional exploration of them but because in the past year I have—almost weekly, and always while looking for something else—come upon one meditation or another about the fearsomeness of death. Jacques Derrida, it turns out, is afraid of death, and in a recent book asks the question "My death— is it possible?" I didn't read on to discover if he thinks it is possible, but I know what my opinion on the subject is (about *his* death, that is). In a book of Arnold Toynbee's reminiscences, which I was consulting for some purpose unrelated to mortality, I found the historian's discussion of a friend in whom the thought of death prompted, um, mortal ter- ror—a fear from which, by the way, Toynbee self-congratulatorily pro- nounced himself free. Julian Barnes's book *A History of the World in Ten-and-a-Half Chapters* contains a description of waking up in the middle of the night with death terrors that I could endorse without alter- ing so much as a comma. (I wonder if it is accidental that all of these works were written by men; for whatever my limited experience is worth, I know of no women who give evidence of suffering from this malady.)

I could list many more of these recurrent reminders of mortality; after a while it got to be funny, in a whistling-past-the-graveyard kind of way. I must admit, though, that I was dismayed to discover how com- mon my fear is—not the fear of death as such, which of course has (shall we say) a certain prevalence, but the particular contours my fear takes. I frowned when I read how perfectly Barnes had delineated my expe- rience. Perhaps having taken some comfort from the apparent peculi- arity of my *Ewigkeitangst*, I resent all the more the apparent banality of my *Todangst*. I guess this is one misery that doesn't love company.

But it was only when I came across William Hazlitt's essay "On the Fear of Death" that I finally decided to stare down this specter. Hazlitt has since become a kind of touchstone for me on this subject, largely because I find the view he claims to take so absurd. Indeed, it was Hazlitt's earnest attempt to dispel his death terrors that led me to real- ize that I most certainly do *not* wish to be relieved of my fear in the way that he counsels.

The key to Hazlitt's argument may be found in the essay's first sentences: "Perhaps the best cure for the fear of death is to reflect that life has a beginning as well as an end. There was a time when we were not: this gives us no concern—why then should it trouble us that a time will come when we shall cease to be?" Now, I simply cannot understand this statement. It is *not possible* to fear the past; to fear is to recognize a present, or anticipate future, evil. No one in California is afraid of an earthquake that has already happened, though the recollection of such a catastrophe may produce shudders or even mental trauma; rather, what people *fear* is what the next one will bring. What Hazlitt's argument suggests to me is that a drowning man will grab hold of any old splinter that floats by, even if it obviously cannot bear his weight.

The English poet Philip Larkin—with whom I will later quarrel— understood this absurdity as well as anyone and summed it up in his devastating poem "Aubade":

> This is a special way of being afraid
> No trick dispels. Religion used to try,
> That vast moth-eaten musical brocade
> Created to pretend we never die,
> And specious stuff that says *No rational being*
> *Can fear a thing it will not feel*, not seeing
> That this is what we fear—no sight, no sound,
> No touch or taste or smell, nothing to think with,
> Nothing to love or link with,
> The anaesthetic from which none come round.

Clearly what Hazlitt seeks, and what most of the commentators on this subject seek, is to dispel by the clear light of reason the great fog of emotion that is our natural response to the contemplation of our own death. Now, that emotion seems to me not only natural but appropriate: death is indeed something to fear. But perhaps that reaction says something about my own cowardly and exaggerated regard for my own continuance. C. S. Lewis, in his autobiographical *Surprised by Joy*, claims that he was converted to theism, if not Christianity proper, without any thoughts of his own immortality; he further claims that in this respect his own experience recapitulated that of the Israelites, whose Scriptures suggest that they were brought into a covenantal bond with Yahweh without hearing a word about whether any of them would live beyond this life. What does it say about me that I find Lewis's story almost impossible to believe? At least this, that I cannot disentangle my thoughts of God from my hopes for eternal life.

Because I am a Christian of a rather conventional sort and therefore not inclined to endorse Larkin's dismissal of "religion," I'm not sure that that inability is something to be regretted. Jesus does promise eternal life to those who follow him, and seems to think of it as a desirable goal and a valid incentive for the pursuit of righteousness. And as the martyr Dietrich Bonhoeffer once wrote, there's no point in trying to be holier than God. (Or, I would contend, in finding more "spiritual" and less grossly literal interpretations of Jesus' promise than the traditional one. I'm not interested in any reconfiguration of the notion of eternal life that doesn't at some point—I don't mind a long sleep—get me out of the grave, and I doubt that many other people are either.)

It's hard to tell what Hazlitt himself believed. He makes a few vague bows in the direction of religion, but that's all, and his arguments seem tailored for the skeptic. But if one believes or even strives to believe in the promise of eternal life, then Hazlitt's desire to reconcile himself to the cessation of all being is obviously inappropriate. Why argue for our reconciliation to a state that our professed creed claims we will never experience? And yet any number of Christian writers have drawn on the same Stoic traditions Hazlitt echoes. The seventeenth-century theologian Jeremy Taylor, in his famous treatise *The Rule and Exercises of Holy Dying*, proclaims, "As our life is very short, so it is very miserable; and therefore it is well it is short." He then goes on for many pages about the innumerable afflictions and miseries of life and the consequent virtue of being relieved of such suffering, without remembering to note that, according to his own creed, the mortal coil that we shuffle off is to be replaced by immortal glory and joy. Montaigne's Stoicism is still more pronounced, as might be expected from a man whose mind was so utterly shaped by the ancients, whatever faith he may nominally have professed, and I have considerable sympathy for Pascal's complaint:

"His completely pagan views on death are inexcusable; for all hope of piety must be abandoned if we are not at least willing to die as Christians." For a Christian or other believer in an afterlife to pursue Hazlitt's and Montaigne's course would amount to an ethically dubious hedging of bets: I believe that I will live forever, but just in case I don't, I had better reconcile myself to rotting in the grave as well. Is it psychologically possible to do both?

Perhaps. When I visited Nigeria a few years ago, I met African Christians who, in times of trial, practice a kind of serial connection of religions: first they visit the church, then they pray in the mosque, and before returning home they stop to pay a priest of the old tribal religion to make sacrifices for them. Just to cover all the bases. If such behavior exhibits a virtue, it is hope rather than faith; but even if we call it hope, we must do so, I think—perhaps my own limitations are at work here, or those of my culture—in a gambler's sense of the word. One, let us be just, becomes a gambler because all other options have failed, or because in his or her world there seems to be no better basis on which to distinguish among the complex and various options; but that is not what I desire for myself. What I want, or rather what I feel I must want, is not a stoical resignation or a series of calculated wagers, but a peaceful contemplative gaze toward my necessary future. Fat chance.

I once wrote something about friendship, and though it may be hard to credit, there were times in the writing that I thought I had a distinctive contribution to make to the subject. The delusion passed, but such dreams are common among writers, and their recurrence seems not at all limited by sober reflection on one's past self-overestimation. I cannot imagine anyone coming to the subject I have been considering in these pages with such high expectations; but the many who nevertheless take it up do so in a spirit of, to adapt a theologian's phrase, ultimate concern. We resemble Coleridge's ancient mariner, whose heart, as long as his tale remains untold, within him burns. And after the telling it burns only a little less.

And so I find myself recalling with nostalgia my childhood apprehension of eternity. That fear, in my case at least, was subject to intellectual manipulation; it could be made to evaporate with a few conceptual adjustments and a little practice in employing them. (It didn't hurt that the alternative to everlasting life is everlasting death.) This fear of death itself, though, shows no sign of being dismissable; can such a demon be extracted even with prayer and fasting? Still, I tell myself as I try to imagine an experience very different from my own, the histories of all creeds, not just Christianity, are filled with accounts of people who looked squarely at death and took it as it came. It is also true that the aged testify to the gradual weakening of life's hold upon them—it was Malcolm Muggeridge, I think, who said that when he reached a certain age he began to feel that he had to *decide* whether to get up in the morning or just die—but this is of course no virtue. As Montaigne wrote in a slightly different context, "Our conscience must reform by itself through the strengthening of our reason, not through the weakening of our appetites. . . . What I owe to the favor of my colic is neither chastity nor temperance." Exhaustion with life is not the courage to face death. Whether one expects to return to dust or to watch one's sins played out in some celestial cinema, Hamlet was indeed right when he said that the readiness is all.

How odd—for me and I suppose for anyone reading—to labor through this bramble of words only to end with a phrase as familiar and common as dust itself, to stumble at the end of one's journey upon a commonplace that had been readily accessible at the journey's beginning. As though to write (to read) were a vigorous and hopeful rubbing at an old brass candlestick, an activity in which one's highest ambition is for recovery, restoration—to know something as it was known, to see it as once we, or someone else perhaps, saw it. What can we *learn* about fear, about death?

5

FRIENDSHIP AND ITS DISCONTENTS

SAMUEL JOHNSON BELIEVED that Burton's *Anatomy of Melancholy* made the finest bedside reading, in the morning as well as the evening, of any book he knew (and he knew a lot of them). C. S. Lewis, in *Surprised by Joy*, reflecting on books that are good to read while eating—which must meet the same standard as bedtime books: the ideal is, in Lewis's words, "a gossipy, formless book that can be opened anywhere"—also chooses Burton, and further recommends Herodotus, Sterne's *Tristram Shandy*, and Boswell's *Life of Johnson*, where, as it happens, you may find the great doctor's endorsement of Burton. I myself have relied over the years on Montaigne's *Essays*, though I am intrigued by Oliver Sacks's choice: some years ago he bought a photocopier so he could have a few pages of the *Oxford English Dictionary* handy for nocturnal perusal. Presumably he feared that lugging even one hefty volume of the *OED* to bed would put him in danger of being crushed to death if he happened to doze off in middefinition.

I find that *The Norton Book of Friendship* presents a stimulating and relatively safe set of opportunities for the bedtime, or mealtime, reader. Eudora Welty (the great Mississippian novelist) and Ronald A. Sharp have collected a galaxy of testimonies to friendship: their volume presents us with letters to friends, poems about friends, and stories that explore the tensions and rewards of friendship, along with the classic explorations of friendship by Aristotle, Cicero, Montaigne, and others. The authors that are represented range from ancient Chinese poets to modern American diplomats. This is a lovely book. It is large in its scope, catholic in its tastes, beautifully bound and printed. It also raises, though perhaps not intentionally, some fascinating and important questions about the definition and the meaning of friendship.

Of course one of the greatest pleasures to be gained from reading a book of this kind derives from compiling a list of omissions. How could Welty and Sharp have possibly neglected James Wright's lovely poem "Arrangements with Earth for Three Dead Friends," certain passages from Rabelais's *Gargantua and Pantagruel*, scenes from the fiction of Austen and Dickens and Tolstoy? Couldn't they have made room (considering their ample attention to epistolary friendships) for some of the letters between those dear friends and great scholars Walter Benjamin and Gershom Scholem? Yet even as I tabulate my missing favorites, I am aware that lists of this kind are always idiosyncratic; it must be the curse of anthologists everywhere to have to listen to cries of protest from readers convinced that their particular tastes have universal appeal.

This being said, however, I must in all seriousness bemoan one very important omission, which seems to me to open the doors to those perplexing questions I referred to earlier: there is no greater and more moving passage about friendship than Augustine's description, in book IV of the *Confessions*, of his "very dear" (but unnamed) friend, an acquaintance from childhood, a fellow student and then fellow teacher of rhetoric. "My soul could not be without him," writes Augustine; and then, recalling his friend's sudden illness and death, "my heart was darkened over with sorrow, and whatever I looked at was death. My own country was a torment to me, my own home was a strange unhappiness."

It is hard for me to believe that so powerful and so famous a testimony to the emotional intensity of which friendships are capable could have been excluded from this anthology by accident or ignorance. Indeed, I am tempted to suspect that the editors left this passage out because it calls into question the very idea of friendship—a broad and vague one, as we shall see—upon which the anthology relies. As soon as Augustine calls this young man his "dear friend," he takes the word back: "But he was not in those early days [of childhood], nor even in this later time, a friend in the true meaning of friendship, because there can be no true friendship unless those who cling to each other are welded together by you [God] in that love which is spread throughout our hearts by the holy spirit which is given to us." What precisely is Augustine saying here? That Christians can have "true friendship" only with other Christians, and that, by extension, Jews can have such friendship only with other Jews, Muslims with other Muslims, and so on? In other words, is he saying that shared religious commitments are necessary for genuine friendship? Or is his position a more radical one, namely that only Christians are capable of genuine friendship, because only they have the indwelling power of the Holy Spirit which alone is capable of breaking down the sin-built barriers between persons?

In either case, I cannot agree. I, a Christian, have what I believe to be real friendships with those who are not Christians; those friendships have certain limitations that are sometimes painful to me, but then the same can be said for my friendships with my fellow Christians. Moreover, I have seen (in this anthology among other places) compelling testimony to friendships between people who are not Christians, or for that matter believers of any kind. Nevertheless, Augustine's strict definition raises an important question: at what point does a cordial, or mutually enjoyable or beneficial, relationship become a friendship? While reading *The Norton Book of Friendship* I remembered a wonderful essay by Joseph Epstein entitled "A Former Good Guy and His Friends." In it Epstein, referring to Plutarch's claim that a person needs no more than seven friends in his or her life, writes,

I can think of exactly seven friends, very good friends, whose death or disappearance from my life would devastate me. I can think of a second tier of ten or so friends who enrich my life but with whom the same degree of easy intimacy and depth of feeling does not quite exist. I can think of a third tier of twenty or so people whom I am always pleased to see or hear from, in whose

company I feel perfectly comfortable, and with whom I believe I share a recip-
rocal regard.

At this point Epstein asks whether the people in this third tier, who
certainly are "more than acquaintances," really should be called
"friends." "There ought to be a word," he suggests, "to denote relationships that fell between that of acquaintance and friend." In fact,
there may be such a word. C. S. Lewis in *The Four Loves* argues that on
a level below genuine friendship—*philia,* which in Greek tradition is
truly a form of love, just as much as *eros* (sexual love) or *storge* (famil-
ial affection)—lies companionship. Perhaps Epstein's third tier is made
up of his companions. Indeed I wonder whether his *second* tier isn't
also made up of companions, if we were to be properly strict in limit-
ing the title of friendship to those whom we love.

In any case, Welty and Sharp aren't the least interested in such
restrictions. If Augustine's rigid definition of friendship is at one end of
the scale, and Lewis's not much closer to the center, Welty and Sharp
stand at the opposite terminus. If Augustine or Lewis had been assigned
to give this book a title, the cover would likely read *The Norton Book of
Companionship, Conviviality, Acquaintanceship, Shared Interests,
Mutual Admiration, Cordial Rivalry, and (Every Once in a While) Genuine Friendship.* And indeed, such a title would be more accurate than
the one the book now bears. T. S. Eliot and Groucho Marx admired each
other's work and got to meet once or twice—Groucho's letter to to his
brother Gummo, describing the inadvertently comic dinner at Eliot's
house during which Groucho wanted to talk about *The Waste Land* and
T. S. about *Duck Soup,* is justly famous—but mutual admiration is not
the same as friendship. Scott Fitzgerald's letters to and about Hem-
ingway, which contain in equal parts flattery and recrimination, suggest merely that two men who are talented in the same field are more
likely to become rivals than friends. Perhaps the oddest entry of all is
the excerpt from the diplomat George F. Kennan's memoirs in which
that longtime student of the Soviet Union recounts his meeting with
Mikhail Gorbachev. It is true that Gorbachev greeted Kennan with surprising grace and warmth, and indeed the whole episode makes a fine

story, but what is it doing in an anthology about friendship? If Catholic-ity-of-Taste were a character in *Pilgrim's Progress* like Valiant-for-Truth, he would occasionally tumble into the Ditch of Incoherence.

It is perhaps not accidental that the examples I have chosen to illus-trate this incoherence are modern ones. The selections from ancient Greece, Rome, and China, along with those from the Renaissance and Enlightenment, clearly conform more closely to Lewis's understand-ing of friendship as a form of love, and to the Aristotelian emphasis on friendship as a virtue, than do most of the modern selections. Now, in the eternal warfare between what the poet W. H. Auden called the Arca-dians and the Utopians—those whose memory constructs an ideal past and those whose imagination constructs an ideal future—I am certainly prone to take the Arcadian side; but even when I remind myself of that prejudice I cannot dismiss the conviction that the more recent selections in this anthology rarely represent anything that deserves to be called friendship, while the older selections often earn that designation.

"Older," "more recent"—where is the dividing line? I am tempted to set it in the middle of the eighteenth century, when the neoclassicism of the Enlightenment was beginning to give way to the Romantic, which is to say the modern, sensibility. Two contrasting letters taken from the anthology will suffice to illustrate the point. Samuel Johnson (who appears in this essay for the second, but not the last, time) had a friend named George Strahan, who feared that he had behaved in such a way as to end his relationship with the great man. Johnson's reply demon-strates in equal measure the classical virtue of magnanimity and the Christian virtue of forgiveness:

> You are not to imagine that my friendship is light enough to be blown away by the first cross blast, or that my regard or kindness hangs by so slender a hair, as to be broken off by the unfelt weight of a petty offence. I love you, and hope to love you long. You have hitherto done nothing to diminish my good-will, and though you had done much more than you have supposed imputed to you my goodwill would not have been diminished.

I write thus largely on this suspicion which you have suffered to enter your mind, because in youth we are apt to be too rigorous in our expectations, and to suppose that the duties of life are to be performed with unfailing exactness and regularity, but in our progress through life we are forced to abate much of our demands, and to take friends such as we can find them, not as we would make them.

These concessions every wise man is more ready to make to others as he knows that he shall often want them for himself; and when he remembers how often he fails in the observance or cultivation of his best friends, is willing to suppose that his friends may in their turn neglect him without any intention to offend him.

When therefore it shall happen, as happen it will, that you or I have disappointed the expectation of the other, you are not to suppose that you have lost me or that I intended to lose you; nothing will remain but to repair the fault, and to go on as if it never had been committed.

Johnson wrote this letter on July 14, 1763. Six years earlier, on December 17, 1756, Jean-Jacques Rousseau had written to a certain Madame d'Épinay, who had attempted to reconcile Rousseau with his former friend Denis Diderot. In this letter Rousseau spends less time dealing with the problem at hand than outlining a kind of position paper on the nature and limits—especially the limits—of friendship.

Since we are discussing this subject, I should like to make a declaration to you as to what I require from friendship, and as to what I desire to exhibit in it in my turn.

Blame freely what you find blameable in my rules, but do not expect to find me easily departing from them; for they are drawn from my disposition, which I cannot alter.

In the first place, I wish my friends to be my friends, and not my masters; to advise me without claiming to control me; to enjoy all kinds of rights over my heart, none over my freedom. I consider those persons very singular who, under the name of friends, always claim to interfere in my affairs without telling me anything about theirs. . . . When [my friend] remonstrates with me, whatever tone he adopts, he is within his rights; when, after having listened to him, I follow my own inclination, I am within mine; and I greatly dislike anyone to keep eternally chattering to me about what is over and done with.

Rousseau goes on in this vein for several hundred more words and concludes: "I require from a friend even a great deal more than all I have just told you; even more than he must require from me, and than I should require from him, if he were in my place, and I were in his." This is as close as Rousseau comes to what he promised at the beginning of this little lecture, what he considers *his* responsibilities in friendship to be.

Though Johnson wrote his letter six years later than Rousseau wrote his, it is clear that Johnson's understanding of friendship belongs (in a truly Arcadian formulation) to the world we have lost, Rousseau's to the world we have inherited. For Johnson, friendship must be cultivated with delicate care and rigorous self-discipline before it can bear fruit: as he once told a friend, "A man, Sir, should keep his friendship in *constant repair*." Youthful pride shuns such discipline, but experienced humility knows that without it there will be no fruit, no sustenance for the spirit. In friendship, as in all else, the incessant demands of the self must be repudiated so that the emotional and spiritual health of the person may be achieved: as Johnson wrote in one of his *Idler* essays, "Those who are angry may be reconciled; those who have been injured may receive a recompense; but when the desire of pleasing and willingness to be pleased is silently diminished, the renovation of friendship is hopeless; as, when the vital powers sink into languor, there is no longer any use of the physician."

But Rousseau, to continue Johnson's medical metaphor, is a kind of anorexic: having consistently refused the nourishment of genuine friendship, fearing some violation of the sleek purity of the imperial self, he lies upon the deathbed congratulating himself for having avoided unhealthy eating. Rousseau's self-deception is immense: he believes that someone can have a claim upon his "heart" without infringing upon his "freedom." What can this mean? *Any* form of human connection compromises one's freedom by bringing another's needs, and often another's suffering, into one's own life; that is the price to be paid for such attachment. Of course, not everyone is willing to pay that price: witness the Buddhist doctrine of nonattachment. But Rousseau will not even admit that a price is to be paid; he insists that he can have the benefits of friendship without having to give anything in return. Such a view of friendship makes friends into nothing more than potentially entertaining shadows passing along the wall of one's personal Platonic cave. A more honest and self-aware man than Rousseau would have acknowledged the isolation that the imperial notion of selfhood always brings: heavy hangs the head that wears the crown. Or as Milton's Satan put it, in a moment of hopefulness that would eventually be shattered, "better to reign in Hell than serve in Heaven." Samuel Johnson, on the other hand, would reject all such formulations: he had lived often enough in the hell of friendlessness to be willing to be George Strahan's servant—which is to say, his friend.

The Romantic cult of selfhood, then, is in large part responsible not only for the scarcity in our culture of real friendship, considered as a love and as a virtue, but also for our general inability to realize that anything is missing. Companionship, and relations more tentative still, may be confused with friendship only when a truly vibrant model of nonerotic, nonfamilial relations cannot be found. Aristotle wrote that no one would wish to live without friends, even if he or she had every other worldly good; but then he had not met Rousseau or his innumerable progeny.

Nevertheless, there are times when harsh circumstances force the imperial self off its throne and demand a reconnection with humanity that makes friendship not only possible but necessary. In this anthology the clearest examples of this situation derive from war, especially World War II: a moving exchange between two German intellectuals living in America, the novelist Thomas Mann and the scholar Erich Kahler; Elie Wiesel's account (from *Night*) of the power of friendship, and of music, on a forced march to Buchenwald. The ideological conflicts of the Cold War make an appearance too, for instance in the letters between the Algerian-French novelist Albert Camus and the Russian writer Boris Pasternak. For these people, enormous sociopolitical conflicts make demands upon us that friendships help us tolerate, balance, and assess. The great Polish-Lithuanian poet Czeslaw Milosz once wrote that in times of terror (he was thinking particularly of the Warsaw Ghetto during World War II) poetry can become "as necessary as bread" because of its power to remind us, in bestial circumstances, of what it means to be human. Friendship clearly can have the same civilizing and reassuring effect.

It should be noted, however, that a peculiarly dangerous counterfeit of friendship may afflict people living in such times. E. M. Forster writes that when one lives in an "Age of Belief"—by which he meant passionate and often closed-minded ideological commitment—one may sustain oneself with "personal relationships." This sounds innocent enough, but in the same essay Forster puts forth the most notorious claim of his long career: "If I had to choose between betraying my country and betraying my friend, I hope I would have the guts to betray my country"—a statement that, forty years later, Sir Anthony Blunt would use to explain why he had chosen to betray his country instead of his "friends" the Soviet spies Kim Philby and Donald Maclean. Here friendship, or more accurately the hatred of bourgeois beliefs and attitudes that bound together these gifted Cambridge men and that was as close as they could come to friendship ("the enemy of my enemy is my friend"), serves to justify the profoundest evil.

In light of these somber reflections, we may wish to reconsider Augustine's suggestions about the relationship between friendship and Christian belief. Unfortunately, *The Norton Book of Friendship* doesn't offer much help. Except for the usual biblical pairings (Ruth and Naomi, David and Jonathan), a Hasidic tale by Elie Wiesel, and a few letters from Dietrich Bonhoeffer to Eberhard Bethge from which one would be virtually unable to tell that either man was a believer, the anthology offers almost no specifically Jewish or Christian pictures of friendship. Before we attribute this state of affairs to bias on the part of the anthologists, we might consider whether Judaism and Christianity have offered significant and sustained reflection on the role of friendship in the spiritual life. Could it be that the West shows a serious interest in friendship only when it emphasizes its classical more than its biblical inheritance?

Indeed Gilbert Meilaender, in his 1981 book *Friendship: A Study in Theological Ethics,* points to a tendency among Christian thinkers (upon whom I will focus, because of my ignorance of Jewish thought on the subject) to see ethical dangers in the "preferential" nature of friendship. Meilaender quotes Jeremy Taylor, the seventeenth-century Anglican divine: "When friendships were the noblest things in the world, charity was little." In other words, when the ancient Greeks and Romans emphasized the great virtue of friendship, they neglected to care for those who stood outside *philia*'s charmed circle. Samuel Johnson, as was his wont, formulated the potential problem with exemplary clarity (though in a way perhaps inconsistent with his own great capacity for friendship): "All friendship is preferring the interest of a friend, to the neglect, or, perhaps, against the interest of others. . . . Now Christianity recommends universal benevolence, to consider all men as our brethren; which is contrary to the virtue of friendship, as described by the ancient philosophers."

Meilaender rightly questions whether Johnson's stating of the problem is wholly accurate—though not, in my view, as aggressively as he might have: he tends to emphasize the potential areas of conflict between *philia* and *agape,* and thus is sympathetic with Johnson's concern, if he does not share Johnson's conclusion. But there is another way to consider the issue. A friend who, for instance, requires me to ignore the needs of the poor and the suffering, to repudiate the commandment of my Savior to aid and comfort them, so that instead I might do his bidding, is likely to be no more capable of genuine friendship than Rousseau. Here the Greek understanding of friendship as dependent upon a shared cultivation of the virtuous life seems not to contradict the Christian message but to suggest the proper boundaries and the proper role of friendship in the pursuit of holiness. I am reminded in this context of a vivid image from Lewis: "Lovers are normally face to face, absorbed in each other; Friends, side by side, absorbed in some common interest."

Nevertheless, when one tries to think of great Christian friendships, few come to mind—to my mind, anyway—and oddly enough, the first two that pop up involve a man and a woman (*The Norton Book*'s friendships, like those in life itself, are almost all same-sex). We have Heloise and Abelard, late in life, when she was an abbess and he an abbot; but of course a great deal of suspicious scrutiny has been given to that friendship, naturally enough in light of their earlier erotic relationship. The same kind of scrutiny has been given to St. Francis and St. Clare, though for much less reason. Bonhoeffer and Bethge were indeed great Christian friends. Augustine and Alypius were close even before they became Christians almost simultaneously. As a teacher of English literature, I also tend to think of George Herbert and Nicholas Ferrar, William Cowper and John Newton (an asymmetrical friendship, thanks to Cowper's profound mental and spiritual afflictions and Newton's attentiveness to them), Flannery O'Connor and her longtime correspondent known only as "A." C. S. Lewis and Charles Williams are candidates, and there is Lewis's troubled and inconsistent friendship with J. R. R. Tolkien. Tractarianism was, as Lewis says in *The Four Loves*, a movement that began in a series of friendships.

Even as I list these, however, I am aware that when Christians become especially close to one another we may not refer to them as friends: we may instead follow the biblical pattern and call them "brothers and sisters in Christ." A true enough naming, but a distinction needs to be made. After all, when Lewis and Tolkien fell out with each other and for all practical purposes ceased to be friends, they did not cease to be brothers in Christ, a point with which both would have been quick to agree. Friendship, as most commentators on the subject have pointed out, is a willed, a chosen thing (otherwise it could not be a virtue); but we do not choose our brothers and sisters in Christ, nor that larger family of all humanity to which we have unalterable obligations. Bonhoeffer and Bethge were brothers in Christ, but they were also friends; each of them had other brothers in Christ who were not friends, and probably friends who were not brothers in Christ.

Such distinctions pose questions that can only be listed here, not answered: How (if at all) do our responsibilities to our Christian friends differ from those we bear toward other brothers and sisters in Christ? If we have unbelieving friends, what happens when our obligations to them conflict with our obligations to our fellow Christians? (As St. Paul says to the Galatians, "Let us work for the good of all, and *especially* for those of the family of faith" [nrsv].) How does our understanding of such friendships change when we see them in the light of biblical commands to proclaim the gospel, to defend our faith, to bear witness to the saving power of Christ?

These questions lead to another, in some ways just as important: Why is Meilaender's book such a curiosity?—which is to say, why are there so few attempts, by Christians anyway, and for all I know by Jews, to formulate a theology of friendship? *The Norton Book of Friendship* came to me first as an entertaining bedtime book, "gossipy and formless" indeed, agreeable and entertaining. But with subsequent readings I have come to think of this book as compelling testimony to a profound cultural poverty. Real friendship, all the authorities agree, has always been rare, but it has often been sought, and celebrated when found. Among the most celebrated of all friendships is that between Michel de Montaigne and Étienne de la Boetie, which lasted only four years before Boetie's untimely death. So deep was Montaigne's grief that, over a period of decades, he wrote his magnificent *Essays* largely as compensation for the wonderful conversations he once had enjoyed but would never have again. In this friendship (and note the present tense in the first sentence) "our souls mingle and blend with each other so completely that they efface the seam that joined them, and cannot find it again. If you press me to tell why I loved him, I feel that this cannot be expressed, except by answering: Because it was he, because it was I." Few people in any age and in any culture have had a friendship like this one; how many people in our world can comprehend, or even imagine, the experience Montaigne describes?

6

SIGNS AND WONDERS

A FEW YEARS AGO I JOINED a group of people who were keeping a lengthy vigil over a dying man. He was a priest and a teacher, a man of great passion, who loved and was loved deeply. Cancer of the bone marrow was racking his body; heavy medication could not hold off the cease-less tides of pain. That he was confined to a hospital bed made every-thing worse. Over a period of weeks we took half-nights with him in an informal rotation, helping him go to the bathroom, bringing him water, but most of the time—if my watch was typical—just sitting in a chair, positioned in the wedge of light that comes from the corridor through the half-opened door, trying unsuccessfully to read. Whenever I looked at him lying in his dim corner of the room I couldn't help thinking that the cancer had made him younger: he was thinner, of course, but not yet wasted, and his hair was rumpled like a boy's. The creases in his face and his mottled skin were obscured by the darkness. I could almost imagine that I was merely sitting up with a sick child, one who would soon recover and resume his games and laughter.

Once, at about two in the morning, he raised his head from the pil-low and looked at me for a few moments. I thought he might be won-dering who was there because he had had so many companions—which may have been reassuring (we hoped so) but was certainly confusing. "Is there anything I can do for you, Joe?" I asked.

"Just pray, Alan," he whispered—so he did know who I was—and laid his head back on the pillow.

I did attempt to pray, of course, leaning forward and closing my eyes, but my concentration lapsed; I was still wondering why he had raised his head to look at me. And I was also wondering—conventionally but inevitably—why this man was suffering so. After a few moments I lifted my own head, and as I did a glint of light pricked the corner of my right eye. I turned and saw, on the table a few feet away, a flower arrangement, from which rose a balloon. The balloon was printed on one side with an absurdly familiar image, a bright yellow smiling have-a-nice-day face; the other side was made of silver foil. It was that foil, caught by the slant of light from the door, that I had seen. Just as I looked up, the barely perceptible currents from the air conditioner touched the balloon; the smiling face, which had been turned toward Joe, now rotated, gravely and formally, until the face was pressed against the wall. If Joe, who was for the moment lying on his back, had opened his eyes, he would have seen the reflection of his broken body in the balloon's cheap and silly mirror.

To a man who wanted his son healed, Jesus said, "Except ye see signs and wonders, ye will not believe." I too desired signs and wonders, but this ludicrous spectacle? It was simultaneously banal and grotesque, or rather grotesque in its banality; it was wholly unsuited to comprehend or to represent the enormity of what was going on in that room; it was what one might expect from the pen of a high school junior in his first creative writing class; above all, it was unworthy of God. Better no sign at all than this foolishness, no answer at all than this travesty of revelation.

My face flushed with resentment, even anger. Thinking back on that moment now, I think what angered me most of all was the transparency of the symbol: any fool could read it. My training as a teacher of literature, which among other things is training in the interpretation of symbols, was scarcely needed here. Still, I found myself elaborating, bringing to bear on a nonexistent hermeneutical problem an array of pointless and common illustrations from Bible, prayer book, and literature. God had turned his back on Joe; the Lord would not make his face shine upon Joe, would not lift up his countenance upon him or give him peace. And if Joe sought to see God's face, he would see only his own sad and ravaged one—however imperfectly, and through a glass (a silver-foil glass) darkly. If he were granted anything, it would be self-knowledge: his battle with cancer was, in the old Greek term, an *agon*, in which the essential contest is not with one's opponent but with oneself and one's limitations.

As such notions marched through my mind—just as they might had I been preparing for a Lit 101 course—I chastised myself for frivolous academicism. But I couldn't help myself; that's the way I think. I recalled Hector and Achilles, facing one another outside the gates of Troy. Hector looks upon the great shield made by Hephaestus, with its images of the civilized world of dance and harvest, law and wine, that world that he loves and that he is about to lose forever, while Achilles stares at his own armor, now worn by Hector, the visible and palpable token of his obsessive commitment to the warrior's calling. *There* were symbols that did justice to the *agon;* in the hospital room where I sat gazing blankly at a cheap balloon were none.

When Joe died almost a month later, his funeral suited me much better. It was held in the spare and stony church where he had ministered for many years; the music was, for the most part, old and beautiful; the liturgy was rooted in the most ancient traditions of the Christian faith. Here at last were the symbols adequate to the event: stone, cross, bread, wine, solemn and resonant words. We seemed appropriately distant from the dismal sterility of that hospital room.

I did not ask, from the onset of my pitiful epiphany to the conclusion of the burial rite, or indeed for a long time afterward, what need Joe had of "symbols adequate to the event" of his illness or what comfort he could have drawn from them. He may have needed them very much or not at all, but I didn't ask. I even forgot to keep wondering why, in one of the nights of his dying, he had struggled to lift his head and look at me. For such neglect I desire his forgiveness.

I desire it because I think differently now from the way I did then. A year after Joe's death, in the same hospital in which he had suffered and I had watched, my wife gave birth to a son. Slowly, then, it came to me that the multitude of cheap and tawdry symbols that accompany American births, as well as American deaths, could do nothing to reduce the dignity and the enormity of the event. As I sat in a room very like Joe's, in a chair indistinguishable from the one in which, however petulantly, I had received my sign, and looked at an oddly familiar arrangement of flowers accompanied by a celebratory balloon, I thought (while struggling to hold my newborn son) that in fact the energy went in the other direction: the event lent its dignity to those symbols and endowed them with a curious weight, a ludic solemnity, that on their own they could have neither possessed nor represented.

After this experience the memory of my absurd revelation no longer brought anger. Now when I remember the reflection of Joe's body in that foil balloon, I still sometimes think of Hector of the shining helm and brilliant Achilles before the walls of Troy, but the distance between the two worlds no longer seems so great, nor the comparison so frivolous.

7

THE REVENGE
OF THE SCROLL

ALBERTO MANGUEL'S RAMBLING, digressive *A History of Reading* is not exactly a history; more accurately, it is a series of often fascinating snapshots. Here we have a lector reading aloud to cigar rollers in a Key West cigar factory; there we have an account of great bibliokleptomaniacs (book thieves); and look, a photograph of Eleanor of Aquitaine's tomb, with its sculpture of Eleanor reclining, a book in her hands. Manguel provides chapters on iconography, translation, forbidden books, and the categorical schemes of libraries. Interspersed with historical commentary are Manguel's reflections on his own life as a devout reader, including his vivid story of the evenings he spent as a teenager in his hometown of Buenos Aires reading aloud to the blind and elderly Jorge Luis Borges.

Manguel is a learned and enthusiastic advocate of reading, and to his credit he disavows at the outset any narrative coherence in the volume. His book, he says, "skips chapters, browses, selects, rereads, refuses to follow conventional order." This language suggests that Manguel formally or structurally imitates how most of us read, and this is arguably appropriate, but his method is too jumpy for my taste. And taste will inevitably be the arbiter in judging a book of this kind, so frankly personal and anecdotal. It's interesting that in *The Gutenberg Elegies*, a plea for the value of reading, Sven Birkerts finds the reading of novels normative and so proceeds to defend a slow, disciplined, linear attentiveness that contrasts strikingly with Manguel's protean fluctuations. When I first read Birkerts I complained about this emphasis, but I now realize that my sympathies are more with him than with Manguel.

Still, I learned a great deal from this historical jumble. Manguel is especially useful on the manifold ambiguities of reading. In a chapter called "Learning to Read" he notes that "in every literate society, learning to read is something of an initiation, a ritualized passage out of a state of dependency and rudimentary communication"; yet he also demonstrates that there have been many different methods of teaching reading, methods shaped not only by the teachers' goals but also by their fears. Some scholars (Socrates in Plato's *Phaedrus* seems to have been the first of these) worry that readers will suffer mnemonic atrophy: why memorize words that one can keep safely stowed on one's shelves—or on one's hard drive? (And indeed, since the invention of the printing press steady rises in literacy levels have been accompanied by steady declines in the ability and willingness to memorize.) Other teachers, however, fear that the young reader will show insufficient reverence for the written word—thus a medieval Jewish ceremony described by Manguel:

> On the Feast of Shavuot, when Moses received the Torah from the hands of God, the boy about to be initiated was wrapped in a prayer shawl and taken by his father to the teacher. The teacher sat the boy on his lap and showed him a slate on which were written the Hebrew alphabet, a passage from the Scriptures and the words "May the Torah be your occupation." Then the slate was covered with honey and the child licked it, thereby bodily assimilating the holy words.

(Manguel does not note the biblical echoes here, especially Psalm 19:10 and Ezekiel 3:3.) A similar reverence led the schoolmen of the medieval universities to approach key philosophical texts by means of commentaries—only the advanced, proven student was worthy to read the classics themselves. On subjects such as these Manguel provides a bag-ful of provocative information.

Now, had I been writing *A History of Reading*—well, the book would have been far less learned, I will be forthright about that. But I would have focused considerable attention on a subject that Manguel treats only briefly: the physical character of books. He does have a chapter called "The Shape of the Book," in which he describes the shift in the Middle East from clay tablets and papyrus scrolls (or, in the case of the Jews, vellum scrolls, a strong preference Manguel doesn't mention) to codexes—sheets of parchment tied together with string, the precursors to our books. But Manguel quickly moves on, sketching the evolution of desks, tables, and chairs designed especially for reading, then drift-ing back to Gutenberg and his press, to the great Italian Renaissance humanist and bookmaker Aldus Manutius—whose volumes remain among the most beautiful ever made—and to British publisher Allen Lane's invention of paperback culture with the first Penguins. But we need an account of reading that takes much more seriously the role that these *objects* we read have in our experience.

For example, how different the Scriptures must have been for Chris-tians when they were literally *ta biblia* ("the little books"—plural), that is, a set of scrolls kept in a pigeonholed cabinet, rather than a bound codex, the Bible (singular). Indeed, the use of scrolls militated so strongly against the emerging commitment of the early church to the unity of all Scripture that scrolls were quickly abandoned. Scholars have found that in the second, third, and fourth centuries A.D., when the great majority of pagan texts were recorded in scrolls, the Bible was almost always preserved in codex form. (Manguel, by the way, mistak-enly thinks that the preference for codexes was universal in the late clas-sical period.) The theologian Stanley Hauerwas has suggested to me that the early church's commitment to the *typological* interpretation of Scripture—in which the Old Testament read as a prefiguring or fore-shadowing of the New—mandated a technology that would bind both together.

This shift from scroll to codex is perhaps the greatest single change in the history of the read object. The mass production that the printing

press made possible may have had an equally significant overall importance, but the experience of reading a hand-copied book is not so dramatically different from the experience of reading a machine-made
one.

Or is it? Even some apparently trivial details of design may be more
significant than we think. Gabriel Josipovici, in *The Book of God*, suggests that "a major reason why the New English Bible was greeted with
such a chorus of disapproval [when it appeared in complete form in
1970] was surely that in most editions it was designed to look just like
any other book." In the years since then we have grown more accus-
tomed to Bibles in a variety of shapes and with a wide range of textual
designs, but then—just a few decades ago—the absence of leather binding, India paper, numbered verses, descriptive page headers, and so on
must have been disconcerting. Most criticism deplored the translation's pedestrian style, but Josipovici's shrewd comment makes one
wonder whether readers' perceptions of that style were shaped by a
"policy of making the Bible look as much like a classical novel as possible"—just as perceptions of the Jerusalem Bible may have been
shaped by *its* "policy of making the Bible look as much like a newspa-
per as possible."

Moreover, all of us purchase and use Bibles with an eye toward
appearances; the size, shape, and design of our Bible transmits messages to us and to those who see us. In college and graduate school I
favored a simple hardbound edition of the Revised Standard Version,
eschewing leather binding as a decorative frivolity. The brightly colored paperbacks preferred by some of my peers I also rejected, though
for the opposite reason: they didn't seem prepared for the long haul;
they lacked sufficient gravitas. (Worst of all was a phenomenon of the
1970s, the Salem Kirban Bible, in which the portions of Scripture
allegedly descriptive of the end times were printed in enormous mul-
ticolored print and surrounded by illustrations, while the remaining 95
percent of God's Word was relegated to almost unreadably tiny letter-
ing and was undignified by commentary.) In the ensuing years I have
come to favor leather-bound but extremely small Bibles, perhaps in
reaction against all those enormous annotated tomes that make me

think of crude spiritual weaponry—as though the Bible were the cudgel rather than the sword of the Spirit.

Certainly Josipovici is right. These matters are important, but I find myself returning again and again to the scroll-codex distinction, in part because we now suspect that the victory of the codex was not permanent. An offhand comment by Manguel opens the issue: "The unwieldy scroll possessed a limited surface—a disadvantage we are keenly aware of today, having returned to this ancient book-form on our computer screens, which reveal only a portion of text at a time as we 'scroll' upwards or downwards." One way in which computer programmers have attempted to rectify this "disadvantage" is by making it easier for us to travel within a given document, and among various documents, by the use of hypertext links that enable rapid transfer to another location. This does, of course, help to counter the intrinsic limitations of screen size—but at what price?

Certainly the faculty of extended attentiveness, so prized by Sven Birkerts, is constantly under attack. How many of us, while reading a lengthy and perhaps difficult text online, can resist repeated invitations (highlighted in brightly colored letters, often underlined, and perhaps even blinking or flexing animatedly) to break our concentration and go somewhere else? And as a corollary to that, hypertext documents beyond a certain length will sacrifice unity to downloading speed. Look at a CD-ROM or online Bible and you will see not a single volume but a screen featuring links, each of which will take you to a book of the Bible. One could argue that these electronic Bibles more closely resemble the divided scroll cabinets of the ancient world than the books with which most of us are more familiar.

It is understandable that Christians would want to render their enormous Scriptures more manageable; indeed, we have always sought to do just that—for instance, by breaking the biblical books into chapters and then into verses. But again, what price easy access? If our system of verse division has caused generations of Christians to think of the Bible as a box of bite-sized spiritual nuggets, any one of which can be consumed without disturbing its immediate neighbors—and indeed this has been the prime effect of verse numbering—should we not be wary of making use of an electronic version of the scroll cabinets firmly rejected by the early church? There is a Law of Unintended Theological Consequences to be considered here.

In any case, this matter of electronic reading deserves closer attention. A company called Voyager has been around for some years, selling videotapes and laser discs of classic movies, along with what I think to be the most inventive CD-ROMs on the market. Their CD-ROM version of *Maus,* Art Spiegelman's brilliant comic-book-style account of his father's experiences in Auschwitz, is a tour de force: it includes not only the full text of the original two-volume *Maus* but also audio commentary by Spiegelman, substantial selections from Spiegelman's taped interviews with his father, Vladek (which provided the foundation for the books), a *complete* transcript of those interviews, videos and still pictures from Auschwitz, various forms of written documentation from the camps, photographic reproductions of Nazi propaganda, and so on. This single disc amply justifies the existence of Voyager.

One of its projects not too many years ago was something called Voyager Expanded Books, one of the first e-book ventures and an instructive one, even though—or perhaps because—it failed. These "books" were available at stores on floppy disk and theoretically could be downloaded, for a lower price, from Voyager's Web site. (I tried many times, on three different computers, to download the books, but with no success.) But in any case, here is what Voyager said, in those halcyon days of a few years ago, about its Expanded Books:

> Voyager Expanded Books are designed to change the way you read. Expanded Books keep the look and features of traditional books, while adding computer-based benefits that enhance reading.... Expanded Books are books published on floppy disks, some of which are now also available online. They contain the complete, unaltered text of the hardcover editions, but cost less. You can load them onto the hard drive of your laptop and read them anywhere: on the plane, at the beach, at bedtime (by the light of the screen). You can navigate through them easily, underline passages, write and save margin notes, copy passages into a notebook and print or export them to another document, dogear or paper clip pages, enlarge or change the typeface, or search for specific words or phrases. Some Expanded Books have features unique to the electronic edi-

tion: call up pictures, sounds, author's annotations and end notes just by clicking on a word.

These are bold claims, and after perusing some of the Expanded Books—John McPhee's four books on geology, the selected stories of Eudora Welty—I am prepared to agree with some of the claims. But not with all of them.

I was immediately drawn, as I read Voyager's pitch, to the apparent solution of a long-intractable problem for married or cohabitating readers, viz., how to read in bed without disturbing the person next to you. The idea of a self-lighted book, like that of an illuminated watch face, is appealing. While miniaturized lights that clip to your book have been commercially successful, I misplaced mine years ago, and I don't know anyone who is happy with them. You can adjust the brightness of a laptop's (or an e-reader's) screen for clear readability without illuminating the room. And there isn't the potentially annoying scratching sound of pages being turned: I use arrow keys to scroll down or up and make nary a sound. However, the positions in which you can read from a laptop are severely limited, because the computer is much larger than the average book, and you need to have the arrow keys readily accessible. The only position that works well for me is lying on my back with the computer resting on my belly, but this gets tiresome after a while. Perhaps the new e-readers, like the Rocket-eBook, will help to solve this problem.

I find that most of my evaluations of the Expanded Books and similar technology tend to take the "yes, but" form: "Yes, I can do x, but that creates problem y." The plusses include the ability to carry a whole library—including reference books—in a package about the size and heft of a hardbound dictionary; to find particular words quickly and easily; to take extended notes with a "notebook" feature, or to make briefer marginal annotations; and to underline with perfect neatness, to employ bold or italic print, and to choose large print at will. On the other hand, Expanded Books require an incredibly expensive delivery vehicle, the computer—and it had better be pretty powerful, or else loading the program, finding particular page numbers, and so on will be quite slow. That computer requires electrical power, either via plug or via battery, and we know how quickly a laptop drains battery power. It is impossible to have books of varied dimensions; all books are precisely the size and shape of your computer or reading device. Moreover, while you might be able to take a computer to the beach or the pool, I would not recommend taking it with you onto an inflatable raft. Nor (and this is a major consideration for some readers) are Expanded Books appropriate for bathroom reading.

Beyond these specific cases, evaluation becomes tricky. Some may find the format conducive to serious scholarly reading: you can underline and boldface text quickly and easily and make the aforementioned extended notes. But like the archaic scroll, the electronic text does not readily lend itself to the checking and comparing of one section against another, unless one has a particular word to search for; and the ability to make such comparisons quickly and easily is essential to careful reading. So I feel seriously constrained as I try to read with scholarly care, but that may be a function of what I'm used to. Someone raised on electronic reading likely would find it difficult to read my way.

Perhaps someday we will carry featherlight laptops about with us as readily as students carry backpacks, and the codex—constructed out of its primitive materials: wood pulp, ink, thread, glue—will seem as archaic as parchment scrolls now seem to us. In that case it will be fruitless to argue about the ease with which the codex reader can compare paragraphs hundreds of pages apart.

Perhaps the only case left to be made for the codex is one that, for me, is the most important of all: the aesthetics, the *feel*, of a bound volume. The most ludicrous claim Voyager made for its Expanded Books is that they "keep the look and features of traditional books." This is true only in the sense that a snapshot of a person keeps the look and features of that person: there is a kind of resemblance, to be sure, but no one I know is two-dimensional or three inches tall. I am thinking not only of the weight and heft of a book (the new readers imitate those features fairly well), but also of a trait possessed by books made on a real *printing press:* one can see, if one looks closely—and this is made easier for me, if I remove my spectacles, by my near-sightedness—the imprint, the indentation the inked letters made as they were pressed into the paper. A book has a much fuller *spatial* existence than an image on a computer screen, and a sculptural form that the screen can never have. Which is why there are people who love books without caring much for reading—books are, for such people, *objets d'art*. And perhaps the future of my beloved codexes lies in the aesthetic realm only.

Nevertheless, Voyager's suggestion about beach reading, I must confess, lingers in my mind as I contemplate my upcoming vacation. And for some reason it's the idea of *nighttime* beach reading that appeals most to me. I conjure up a picture of myself reclined in a chaise on the sands, the moon glowing dimly on the surf, my laptop open before me as I read—well, not John McPhee on geology. I'll have to come up with the right thing. Certainly not (for reasons already noted) an electronic Bible. The whole of Proust on a single machine, though—*that's* an appealing prospect.

But then, I consider, to realize that prospect I would have to bring my laptop on vacation. And that would mean having access not just to the screen but also to the keyboard and Microsoft Word. In short, I would be presented with a constant temptation to do some of the work that otherwise would simply pile up until my return to the office. With a sigh of regret I zip the computer in its case and stow it under the desk. Would a Rocket-eBook serve my turn, then? Alas, at the very thought an image comes unbidden to my mind: my sleeping form on a chaise lapped by water, the Rocket-eBook, fallen from my loosened grasp, being borne away by the tide . . .

Too much anxiety accompanies these technophilic fantasies. I hold in my hand an old paperback of one of Trollope's novels and feel my pulse begin to slow and regulate itself. For me, the warm familiarity of the codex will always mean peace.

8

IT AIN'T ME, BABE

As I first said, it's a privilege and an honor and a courtesy at this time and at this age to be able to confront you with something that may perhaps go down in your hearing and may be in history after I'm gone.

—legendary Delta bluesman Skip James, in concert, circa 1967

1.

IN THE YEAR OF THIS BOOK's publication Bob Dylan will be sixty years old. This does not seem very strange to me—not nearly as strange as the fact that, had he lived, John Lennon would have turned sixty last year, or that Paul McCartney will do so next year. Lennon and McCartney represented what came to be called, in the decade of the Beatles, "youth culture." Dylan may have appealed to many young people, but ultimately the sources of his power were to be found elsewhere: he never spoke as a young man but rather as the custodian of ancient traditions. From his first arrival in New York City when he was still a teenager, he may have looked absurdly young, but he was clearly an old soul: all his songs said so. When, in 1967, Dylan retreated to a rented house in upstate New York with the group of musicians who would later be known as The Band, he so deeply immersed himself in country, gospel,

and blues songs that no one around him could differentiate Dylan's
own work from those old tunes. As Robbie Robertson, The Band's gui-
tarist and chief songwriter, told Greil Marcus, "He would pull those
songs out of nowhere. We didn't know if he wrote them or remembered
them. When he sang them, you couldn't tell." The songs Robertson
refers to, or many of them anyway—some written by Dylan, some by
his troubadour predecessors, some by no identifiable person—were
released in 1975 (and repeatedly, before and after, in various bootleg
versions) as *The Basement Tapes*, and they are the subject of Marcus's
book *Invisible Republic*.

It is an amazingly bad book, filled with page after page of wobbly
ramblings in Kerouac-purple prose. The style is supposed to be hip and
allusive; Marcus intends to impress us with his range of cultural reference and what he must think of as the panache with which he offers it.
But what we really get are huge chunks of prose that collectively constitute the best argument yet for the abolition of American Studies programs. Here's an example chosen almost at random from Marcus's
hermeneutically overdriven reading of a couple of lines from Dylan's
song "Lo and Behold!" ("The coachman . . . asked me my name / I give
it to him right away, and I hung my head in shame"):

> "And he asked me my name," the singer remembers; as he spins the incident
> back, he can feel how he'd pulled away, and underneath the worry that's how
> he sings it, a cold half smile on his face, his fish-eye all over the coachman's
> mug. . . .

> His name? He's not supposed to have to tell his name. Suddenly all his con-
> fidence is gone, as if the seat holding his back has fallen away like the chorus
> giving up its last word. Now he is faced with a demand that goes just past the
> endlessly rehearsed gestures of fellowship and distance, acknowledgment
> and evasion, that in 1835, in *Democracy in America*, Alexis de Tocqueville
> caught as the very stuff of a democratic walk down the street of the American
> small town—"that same small town in each of us," as Don Henley could still
> imagine in 1989, in "The End of the Innocence."

Let me make one thing perfectly clear: I will not at this time object
in principle to the citing of Tocqueville and a former member of the

Eagles in the same sentence. Rather, I object to the fatuousness of this *particular* sentence. Don Henley aside, Marcus's references to popular music are usually well chosen and appropriate, but his invocations of American "high" culture (Tocqueville, John Winthrop, Michael Wigglesworth, Lincoln's second inaugural address) are another matter, since they all seem to come straight from *The Norton Anthology of American Literature*. Was there any chance that Jonathan Edwards, whose portrait may be found on the back of the dust jacket of *Invisible Republic*, would be referred to here as anything other than the author of "Sinners in the Hands of an Angry God"? As a cultural historian, Marcus is a rock skimmer rather than a scuba diver.

Perhaps the most distressing moment in the book comes when Marcus quotes this passage from the "I Have a Dream" speech of Martin Luther King Jr.:

> I have a dream that one day every valley shall be exalted, and every hill and mountain shall be made low, and the rough places will be made plain, and the crooked places will be made straight, and the glory of the Lord will be revealed and all flesh shall see it together.

Marcus's purpose in quoting these words—from what he calls, with no qualification, a "political speech"—is to identify them as representing the height of American rhetorical eloquence and then to claim, "That was the faith of the folk revival." (The folk revival?) Now, to be sure, there was genius in King's use of these words for the purposes of that portentous hour; but Marcus seems not to know that credit for the eloquence should go in roughly equal measure to the prophet Isaiah and the translators appointed by King James I. Apparently Marcus was too busy celebrating the folk revival ever to make it to a performance of Handel's *Messiah*.

Marcus has always had a propensity for stylistic hyperinflation and intellectual woolliness, but it has worsened as he has gotten older. It only occasionally afflicted his early and fascinating *Mystery Train: Images of America in Rock and Roll Music* (1975)—which has an excellent chapter on The Band—but it made *Lipstick Traces: A Secret History of the 20th Century* (1989) almost unreadable and *Dead Elvis: A Chron-*

icle of a Cultural Obsession (1991) only scarcely less so. Today one can say of Marcus's writing what Mark Twain said of Wagner's music: it has some wonderful moments, but some absolutely dreadful quarters of an hour. This decline is a shame, because if Marcus could either discover the virtues of editing or cut back on the caffeine and sugar, he would be a fascinating commentator on the contemporary scene at least. In *Invisible Republic* his instincts always lead him in the right direction, even if they can't make him keep his verbal car on one side of the double yellow line.

Above all, he understands both the centrality of Dylan to American culture and the centrality of *The Basement Tapes* to Dylan. Sometimes brilliantly, Marcus traces Dylan's summer in the house called Big Pink back through Harry Smith's enormously influential 1952 collection *Anthology of American Folk Music* ("Smith's *Anthology* is a backdrop to the basement tapes. More deeply, it is a version of them, and the basement tapes a shambling, twilight version of Smith's *Anthology*"), back to figures like the Carter Family, Clarence Ashley, and Dock Boggs, and then farther back into a folk culture bereft of names. Of the basement recordings Marcus writes, "The stronger the songs get, the older they feel," and this is the most important thing to say about them. No wonder Robbie Robertson couldn't tell whether Dylan had just written "Tears of Rage," "You Ain't Goin' Nowhere," and "I Shall Be Released," or had found them. As Elvis Costello once said, "I think he was trying to write songs that sound like he's just found them under a stone."

But the songs from the summer in Big Pink's basement aren't the only Dylan songs that sound that way. That's how his career began, with covers of old songs and with "new" songs that aren't really new at all: "Girl from the North Country" is obviously a take on "Scarborough Fair," while "Blowin' in the Wind," as Marcus notes, takes its melody from a song sung by runaway slaves in the mid-nineteenth century. And from time to time in Dylan's career he has found it necessary to reconnect himself with those folk traditions, sometimes just by following their styles, structures, and patterns of instrumentation, as in that landmark of American music *Blood on the Tracks* (1975), but sometimes simply by recording some great old songs that he hadn't written. Fans were puzzled and frustrated when he did it the first time, in the country standards of 1970's *Nashville Skyline;* perhaps they were more used to the idea by the time he did *Good As I Been to You* (1992) and the especially potent *World Gone Wrong* (1993), which contained all old folk and blues classics. After all, by then, as we will later see, there was reason to think that good things would come from such a return to the sources. *Ad fontes!*

2.

In Dylan the prophet meets the bluesman; the ancient laments of Israel rejoin songs born in slavery and the cotton fields. From this vantage point it seems that it should have been obvious—though of course it wasn't—that Bob Dylan would become not just a monument of popular culture but also a key figure in the social history of American religion.

Popular culture, folk culture, mass culture—these are terms that need discriminating usage. The "folk" for whom the early Dylan spoke were scarcely the working classes, though they envied the workers' authenticity; they were instead the disaffected and confused children of the middle classes, children who certainly felt their own *in*authenticity. If they pretended to intellectuality, as many of them did, they read their own situation in Sartre's accounts of living by "bad faith," in Holden Caulfield's protests against "phoniness," in the beats' determination to leave bad faith behind by going "on the road." Some historians write as if real folk or popular culture can be achieved only by the illiterate and oppressed, but the bourgeoisie can have their unofficial and unsanctioned mythologies too. Dylan came to incarnate one such myth, and he did so by drawing on musical forces that came from way down and way back in American history. As Sister Rosetta Tharpe once said, "There's something in the gospel blues that's so deep the world can't stand it."

The tone Dylan assumed was that of the prophet; his characteristic genre was the jeremiad, though his more popular early songs tended to soft-pedal the wrath a bit: "Blowin' in the Wind," "The Times They Are A-Changing." Some critics have associated the outrage typical of the early Dylan with his Jewishness, but as historian Sacvan Bercovich has argued, the jeremiad has been deeply embedded in American culture since its origins. To condole the innocent downtrodden and condemn their wicked oppressors, preferably in a very loud voice, has for much of our country's history been a highly favored and much-relished practice. Few have done it with more flair than Dylan.

Early on he was celebrated in the *New York Times*, and the managers shook out their moldy wings and descended. Certainly Dylan profited by their attentions and came thereby to believe all the more firmly in his prophetic stature and in the righteousness of whatever cause he happened to be promoting. Would he have indulged in pretentiously obscure symbolism and two-bit surrealism, as he did so often in the mid-1960s, had he not been surrounded by the professional sycophants of the record business? Perhaps not, but Dylan's later history suggests that his self-confidence needed no external support. He quickly showed that he was determined whenever possible to reinvent himself in ways that drove the managers batty. His notorious decision, in July 1965, to "go electric," at the highly publicized Newport Folk Festival no less, infuriated his most dedicated fans—Marcus details their consternated cries of betrayal and hatred—and it was to be only the first of many such occasions. There is no doubt that Dylan has repeatedly been used and invoked by the purveyors of mass culture, but he has also repeatedly sought to remain faithful to some conception of his calling that evades the constrictions of the managers.

From the distance of two decades, the 1975 recording *Blood on the Tracks* seems to mark a crossroads not only in Dylan's career but also in the self-understanding of the generation for whom he was, and perhaps still is, an icon. It is arguably Dylan's finest musical achievement and, as I have said, surely a landmark of American music. This record came at a curious juncture in Dylan's career. He had made a success of his transition to amplified music; he had lost some of his earliest fans but probably gained more new ones. Then in 1966 he was in a serious motorcycle accident, the details of which are still not known, and disappeared from the music scene for more than two years. When he returned, some of his authority seemed to have left him: while he produced some fascinating music (including the basement recordings), he failed to capture audiences or critics as he once had. Through the early 1970s he continued to make records, but their critical reception and sales never matched those of his earlier music. Scarcely more than a decade after his first appearance in New York City, Dylan seemed to many observers to be (for all practical purposes) finished. And indeed in those days ten years seemed to be the extreme limit of rock-and-roll careers; almost no one even hoped to last so long.

Then came *Blood on the Tracks*. For a singer who had so often emphasized political causes or symbolic obscurity, its songs were for the most part astonishingly personal. Dylan's marriage was disintegrating, and though he has always repudiated autobiographical interpretations of the record's songs, the listener cannot help connecting the music with that event. Several of the songs are more simple and direct in their emotional expression than anything Dylan had ever written. And yet something much more than the idiom of confessional love song is going on here; the stakes throughout the record seem much higher.

Dylan had returned to his native Minnesota to record many of these songs, had sought out local musicians, and had avoided electric instruments; a back-to-the-roots imperative was clearly at work. But one gets the impression that Dylan did not feel that he and he alone needed such self-examination and retrenchment; perhaps his whole generation needed it. The harshest song on the album, "Idiot Wind," is reminiscent in some ways of some of Dylan's contemptuous insult-songs of the 1960s: "It's a wonder that you still know to breathe," he sneers. But in the end Dylan condemns himself just as fully and just as bitterly, as the song's "you" metamorphoses into the first-person plural: "We are idiots, babe; it's a wonder we can even feed ourselves."

The song is a powerful one, and it is admirable that Dylan so forthrightly includes himself among the idiots he chastises; but one recognizes here the screechy tones of a Jeremiah who knows what to condemn but who has lost contact with the truth on behalf of which the condemnation is to be proclaimed. What alternative is there to idiocy? One might have expected the Dylan of a decade earlier, or your average sixties radical halfway into a new decade, to denounce Nixon (whose resignation dance was being performed as Dylan recorded these songs) as an idiot, while claiming for himself or herself the sagacity necessary to rule a nation; but here there is no assertion of privileged wisdom. A decade earlier Dylan had given a radical political organization its name when he wrote these words: "You don't have to be a weatherman to know which way the wind blows," but now all he knows is that the wind is an idiot wind, blowing through a nation of vacuous heads.

I contend that Dylan had the intelligence and the honesty to conclude that the self-confidence and self-righteousness of the sixties radicals for whom he had once spoken were utterly misplaced, and further, that he could offer nothing with which to replace them. Lionel Trilling once wrote, shrewdly, that "the modern self is characterized by certain habits of indignant perception." But Dylan, I think, came to understand that indignation is not enough. And in light of his personal pain and of his generation's confusion, there was no need to be surprised when, about five years later, it became known that Bob Dylan had become a Christian.

I was a young Christian myself at that time, as well as a big Dylan fan, and it is hard for me to express how confirmed and sustained I felt by Dylan's conversion, or how infinitely laughable I felt the widespread outrage and disbelief to be. When Dylan's first Christian record, *Slow Train Coming*, was released, Jann Wenner, the founder and editor of *Rolling Stone*, would trust none of his writers with the review but instead wrote it himself. I smirked for weeks over Wenner's ingenious attempts to argue that the record didn't *prove* that Dylan was a Christian, over his desperate protests that songs like "I Believe in You" and "When He Returns" didn't *necessarily* refer to Jesus. I saw Dylan perform on his first tour after his conversion; he had already been greeted by boos and whistles on earlier stops on the tour (just as he had been when he went electric), and when I entered the auditorium people were handing out anti-Christian pamphlets. But I smiled through it all because Dylan and I were on the same side. (I should note that most of the audience that night, in my Bible-belt hometown of Birmingham, Alabama, were on that side too; he got rousing cheers and seemed genuinely to appreciate the warmth of his reception.) Perhaps for the first time, the prophetic voice had discovered a genuine source.

What does Dylan believe today? No one really knows. He has clearly reconnected himself with his Jewish heritage in some manner, a movement attentive fans noted even in the early 1980s: the back cover of his great 1983 recording *Infidels*, which contains a passionately Zionist song called "Neighborhood Bully," shows him squatting and staring at the ground, the buildings of Jerusalem spread out behind and below him. But while he has ceased to write Christian songs, he has never repudiated what he wrote then: "Maybe the time for me to say that has come and gone," he said a few years ago, but also, "Whoever was supposed to pick [that message] up" did so. About this, as about so much else, Dylan has for the most part remained evasive.

The questions about Dylan's beliefs have intensified in the past few years, in the aftermath of a much-publicized heart ailment that had him hospitalized for a while. "I thought I was going to see Elvis," he said soon after being released from the hospital, a remark that in its substitution of Elvis for Jesus is both a witty reflection on American culture's uncertainty about the identity of the true King and a tantalizing comment on Dylan's own religious pilgrimage. Asked a few months later about his beliefs, Dylan gave virtually identical answers to Jon Pareles of the *New York Times* and David Gates of *Newsweek:*

> Here's the thing with me and the religious thing. This is the flat-out truth: I find the religiosity and philosophy in the music. I don't find it anywhere else. Songs like "Let Me Rest on a Peaceful Mountain" or "I Saw the Light"—that's my religion. I don't adhere to rabbis, preachers, evangelists, all of that. I've learned more from the songs than I've learned from any of this kind of entity. The songs are my lexicon. I believe the songs.

That's from *Newsweek;* to Jon Pareles he also invoked Hank Williams's great country gospel song "I Saw the Light" and added, "I've seen that light too."

These comments are as straightforward as we are likely to get from
Dylan—indeed some people will think them unambiguous, though for
an evangelical like me there remains the desire to say, "That's great,
Bob, but tell me what you think about Jesus. Do you accept him as your
Lord and Savior?" To that question I don't think I would get an unam-
biguous answer.

In any case, Dylan's first record of original songs in seven years, 1997's
Time out of Mind, amply justifies his claim that the old songs are his "prayer
book" and "lexicon"—and moreover, it confirms the hypothesis that when
Dylan immerses himself in the world of what he used to call "historical-
traditional music" something powerful is likely to eventuate later on. Every
song on *Time out of Mind* is deeply, deeply saturated in that ancient music.
Perhaps the strongest song on the record, "Trying to Get to Heaven,"
directly quotes as many as a dozen old songs from several genres: country gospel ("I've been walkin' that lonesome valley"), mainline American
folk music ("I was ridin' in a buggy with Miss Mary Jane"), even bluegrass
("I'm just goin' down that road feelin' bad"). And then of course there's
Dylan's self-citation, the echo in the song's refrain ("I'm just tryin' to get
to Heaven before they close the door") of a secular hymn that has already
entered the pantheon, and that he sang for Pope John Paul II in Bologna
in September 1997: "Knockin' on Heaven's Door."

So *Time out of Mind* is deeply, powerfully, self-consciously traditional, but it is also the most emotionally naked Dylan record since
Blood on the Tracks. It is this nakedness that Dylan himself seems to
think most noteworthy about the record: "I don't think it eclipses anything from my earlier period"—as if the wild and unpredictable rides
Dylan gave his listeners for the previous thirty-five years collectively
constitute merely the "earlier period"!—"but I think it might be shocking in its bluntness." Some reviewers have complained that the songs
lack the poetic resonance and metaphorical exuberance of what they
think of as Dylan's best work, but to Dylan this is just the point: "There
isn't any waste. There's no line that has to be there to get to another
line. There's no pointless playing with someone's brain." This direct-
ness is evident in song after song, line after line, and as Dylan himself

acknowledges, sometimes the effect is "spooky": "There's not even room enough to be anywhere," he croaks in "Not Dark Yet."

But flashes of hopeful light occasionally illuminate this dimming landscape. Dylan is still trying to get to heaven before they close the door, and at one point he sings, "I know the mercy of God must be near." It's just that the road is long and hard, and it goes right through the middle of that lonesome valley. *Time out of Mind*'s remarkable combination of unsentimental, unindulgent honesty and deep historical sense makes almost everything else in today's pop music seem trivial and small in comparison. Every rock star with pretensions to seriousness should be locked in a room with this record playing for a solid week (or, in Bono's case, a month): this would be a tonic and restorative for the popular music scene.

But Bob, really, what *do* you think about Jesus?

3.

In 1991, when *Rolling Stone* interviewed Dylan on the occasion of his fiftieth birthday, he gave a curious response when the interviewer asked him if he was happy.

> He fell silent for a few moments and stared at his hands. "You know," he said, "these are yuppie words, *happiness* and *unhappiness*. It's not happiness or unhappiness, it's either blessed or unblessed. As the Bible says, 'Blessed is the man who walketh not in the counsel of the ungodly.'"

It is pleasurable to contemplate the reaction of the typical *Rolling Stone* subscriber to that comment. Here, at least, is a voice connected to something more than the speaker's conviction of his own virtue. For a long time now Dylan has reminded his generation, and anyone else who cares to listen, that the enormous self-confidence they had in the sixties proved to be misplaced: the self that trusts in the righteousness of its own "indignant perception" must eventually discover that it does not inhabit a house of many mansions, but rather a place in which there's not room enough to be anywhere.

Not long ago I saw Dylan play a brilliant and energetic set of music, with several songs from *Time out of Mind*. Some Dylan fans thought it the best show of his they'd ever seen, and I wasn't inclined to argue. Still, I find myself thinking back to the mid-1990s, to a show at the Riviera Theater in Chicago: then too he played with force and energy, though perhaps less joy, for two full hours—something he doesn't always do—but I think what I will remember best is his encore. Returning to the stage, he played a song from the 1989 recording *Oh Mercy*, "What Good Am I?" The song concludes with these words:

> What good am I if I say foolish things
> If I laugh in the face of what sorrow brings
> If I just turn my back while you silently die
> What good am I?

I thought these would be Dylan's last words to his audience; and they would have been good ones. But he played one more song, one from the sixties that, in light of the messages he has been preaching for fifteen years now, and in light of the roles that so many have wanted him to play for so long, took on a new meaning that seemed even more fitting:

> It ain't me, babe
> No, no, no, it ain't me, babe
> It ain't me you're looking for, babe.

9

IN ON THE KILL

On public television and on several educational cable channels the current rage seems to be for documentaries depicting animals eating other animals. To judge by the number of ads inviting people to mail-order videotapes of such predation, even the regularly scheduled programming doesn't offer enough carnage for the viewing audience. And a recent Discovery Channel series, *Walking with Dinosaurs,* relies on amazingly sophisticated computer-generated animation to present dinosaurs largely doing one thing: eating other dinosaurs. Watching it, I found myself wondering how many hours of labor went into even a single brief scene in which the entrails of one creature dangle realistically from the jaws of another.

But I have found that whenever I point out our fascination with animal predation, nearly everyone I talk to quickly—dare I say "automatically"?—defends such shows, and their arguments almost always use the same terms: the old nature shows tended to sanitize and prettify the animal world, disguising from us the harsh truth of a "nature red in tooth and claw." These newer documentaries merely represent to us The Way Things Are, and to the degree that they do so, they are beyond reproach.

Now the very universality of this argument is enough to create suspicion, and indeed it will not bear much scrutiny. It is true that predation is part of The Way Things Are, but sleeping is even more a part of The Way Things Are. For every hour a lioness spends hunting she spends a dozen or more sleeping, yet our television documentaries picture few somnolent cats. And the hard, slow work that hunting chiefly amounts to is given insignificant representation in comparison to the moment at which the claws catch the antelope's side or the teeth tear its neck. Moreover, animals who eat also defecate, yet I cannot remember seeing our intrepid documentarians exploring *that* subject with telephoto lenses and extreme slow motion.

We cannot plausibly claim that any nature documentary merely presents to us an unedited version of The Way Things Are. Filmmakers give us pictures of predation because they, and we, are *interested* in predation. We would rather watch a female praying mantis eat the head of her mate in the midst of copulation (to cite a scene replayed endlessly in nature shows) than watch a caterpillar eat a leaf. The Discovery Channel is just as market-driven as the local news with its "if it bleeds it leads" policy—the market is just a little more specialized—and its programming executives show animals tearing apart the bodies of other animals because the Nielsen ratings and the focus groups indicate the financial wisdom of doing so. There is no other reason. But the question that remains is, what does it say about us that we like to watch such things?

Such shows are, I believe, the modern equivalent of bear baiting, or the educated middle-class equivalent of cockfighting, only with several insulating layers between the viewers and the violence they endorse:

1. We're just watching what others have filmed.
2. They're just filming what the animals are doing.
3. The animals are just following their instincts (by which we really mean, as C. S. Lewis pointed out, "we have no idea why the animal is doing that").

This kind of argument is made possible by what Stanley Milgram called "the fragmentation of the total human act." Milgram's famous experiments on obedience to authority revealed that people can justify participating in the most dreadful deeds if an authority commands their involvement and if they do not directly and physically carry out the acts themselves. They then can understand themselves as being caught up in a chain of events over which they have no control, being neither initiators nor executioners. It seems to me that the modern display of what I call nature's pornography is analogous: because we are neither the ones who kill nor the ones who film the killing, we are merely innocent bystanders with no moral stake in the events we watch. But I believe that by continuing to watch such programs we endorse, affirm, what happens in them. We come to bear a certain responsibility for them. We have not simply failed to turn off the TV; our sin is not merely one of omission. By watching we *will* the continuation of such shows and hence, inevitably, the acts represented in them.

Dante understood this peculiarity of human character perfectly well. As the pilgrim and his guide Virgil visit the eighth circle of hell, the tenth *bolgia* ("ditch" or "pouch") of that circle, they meet the Falsifiers. Among these sinners are a counterfeiter named Master Adam and a falsifier of words, the infamous Greek Sinon, who tricked the Trojans into allowing the fatal wooden horse into their city. Dante watches as Master Adam and Sinon fall into a bitter exchange of insults and vituperation. For thirty lines of verse they snarl at one another, Dante (and we the readers) attending all the time. Then Virgil, the personification of human reason, turns to Dante and says, "Now keep on looking a little longer and I quarrel with you." Why is he troubled? Because, as he later explains, "the wish to hear such baseness is degrading." There are certain events and actions, Virgil seems to say, toward which the only proper response is to avert one's eyes.

This is not a denial of reality, or need not be: in fact, it is an acceptance that reality is often terrible. Predation is, of course, not "base"; it is unlike the bitter recriminations of Sinon and Master Adam in that there is no sin in it. But I cannot think of it as a good thing that some creatures live only by the dying of other creatures, and still less can I think a fascination with such killing good.

Here I must confess my sympathy for the old Christian view that predation is a consequence of the fall. There is, of course, nothing that most people would call "evidence" for this view—though there could be an interesting conversation about what evidence for something like that might be—but I am powerfully drawn to the notion nonetheless. Perhaps this just indicates my limited theological imagination, but though I know about the release of endorphins and the other biochemical mechanisms that reduce or eliminate the pain of traumatic injury (for us as well as for animals), I cannot conceive of the whole structure of predation as something ordained by God from the beginning.

The Puritans seem to have been distinctive in their time for stressing the link between predation and the fall. The historian Macaulay famously sneered that the Puritans banned bear baiting not because it gave pain to the bear but because it gave pleasure to the spectators, but despite its wit this is a morally obtuse comment. The truth is that the Puritans cared about both bears and spectators, as is clearly shown in Keith Thomas's great book *Man and the Natural World*. Thomas reports that the seventeenth-century English writer Philip Stubbes asked in his *Anatomy of Abuses*, "What Christian heart can take pleasure to see one poor beast to rend, tear, and kill another?" Bear baiting is "a filthy, stinking and loathsome game" because it willfully seeks and takes pleasure in the destruction of animals who "are good creatures in their nature and kind"—even though bears in particular "be bloody beasts to mankind and seek his destruction"—animals who are "made to set forth the glory and magnificence of the great God, and therefore for his sake [are] not to be abused."

But if mere respect for creation enjoins our charity to animals, our responsibility is redoubled by the repercussions of the fall of Adam and Eve for the natural order—the world that, as St. Paul says to the Roman church, "has been groaning in travail" because human sinfulness has placed not just us but also it in "bondage to decay." The fall is one of the reasons the viewing of cruelty is nearly as bad as the perpetration of it. Thomas records the eloquently admonitory words of one of Stubbes's contemporaries, a gentleman named John Spencer whose brother had a fascination for cockfighting: "You make that a cause of your jollity and merriment which should be a cause of your grief and godly sorrow, for you take delight in the enmity and cruelty of the creatures, which was laid upon them for the sin of man." I cannot write half so well, or so wisely, so I had best let Spencer's few words stand for hundreds of my own. But it is worth noting that certain forms of untrained animal behavior tend to make me question the "they're just following their instincts" argument and to give renewed consideration to Spencer's "archaic" view of a morally charged nature. For instance, researchers have recently discovered that some male gorillas murder infant gorillas so as to free their mothers from child care and for sexual activity. A book by the British biologist Lyall Watson, *Dark Nature: A Natural History of Evil*, relates tale after tale of just this sort, many worse than the example I just gave. Reading Watson's gruesome litany—and considering his utter inability to think of anything to do about the scenes of horror he describes—I am reminded of the great question of Voltaire's Candide. After hearing his tutor Pangloss recount in gory detail a series of disastrous and bloody experiences, Candide asks, "What a strange genealogy, Pangloss. Isn't the Devil at the root of it?"

There may at times be reasons for us to force ourselves to look at the killing and eating of animals by other animals (just as there may be, and indeed are, good reasons for forcing ourselves to watch films of the Nazi concentration camps). But if we do not *have* to force ourselves, if we look upon such scenes with pleasure and fascination, something is dreadfully wrong. Those who can look without flinching upon animals having the flesh of their bellies eaten while they are still alive are morally numb; those who seek out such scenes for their viewing enjoyment are depraved.

It has occurred to me at several points in the writing of this essay that I should become a vegetarian before having it published. But I am not a vegetarian. I am like the boy of the far North depicted in Galway Kinnell's great poem "To Christ Our Lord," who ventures out into the snow, shoots a goose, and brings it home to be cooked for Christmas dinner. As a long-winded thanksgiving is said by an adult at the head of the table, the boy looks at what he has killed and considers that in a terrible sense it is a creature's death for which thanks are being given. "Is it fitting to eat this creature killed on the wing?" But then it begins to dawn on the boy that the feast of Christmas itself commemorates the begin-

ning of an earthly life whose violent ending is for all Christians the cause
of measureless thanksgiving:

> He asked again,
> For whom had Love stirred?
> Then the Swan spread its wings,
> Cross of the cold North, the pattern
> And the mirror of the acts of earth.

Cygnus the Swan, or the Northern Cross. A bird, a cross; two deaths
converge, represented by a single constellation.

Kinnell says of the boy, "He ate as he had killed, with wonder." He
was right to feel such wonder. But I think that wonder is not enough.
As we contemplate not just the death that redeems but also all those
other deaths—the young zebra raked by the lioness's claws, the field
mouse locked in the owl's talons, and, yes, the cow driven through the
metal chute into the slaughterhouse—that, however necessary to the
natural economy, redeem nothing, we need more than wonder. We
need pity and fear: pity for the animals and fear for ourselves, lest before
the judgment seat we stand accused of complicity in a sad, if quotidian, violence. If we must watch them die, let us do so in that pitying and
fearful spirit, not in the spirit of the documentarian, with slow-motion
replays and telephoto lenses and the expectant leaning forward toward
the glowing screen.

10

LEWIS AT 100

A FEW YEARS AGO I was visiting the campus of Westmont College, an evangelical Christian school in Santa Barbara, California. When I came to the English department, my guide gestured toward a large piece of furniture that stood against one wall of the main office. "And that, of course," he said with a wry smile, "is the *real* wardrobe." He didn't need to explain further—didn't need to specify that he meant the wardrobe the Pevensie children passed through into Narnia in the first of C. S. Lewis's children's books, *The Lion, the Witch and the Wardrobe*. And the wry smile? That was because he knew that my own institution, Wheaton College in Illinois, also claimed to possess "the real wardrobe"—or at least a wardrobe once owned by the Lewis family, which interested parties were free to infer had inspired the famous tale—along with the master's old writing desk, his dining table, and other numinous objects.

What immediately came to mind as I surveyed that obviously fraudulent Californian armoire were the Italian churches that have bickered for centuries over which of them houses the real bones of St. Luke. Will Lewis memorabilia proliferate like relics of the early church until—just as in Italy alone there are enough nails from the True Cross to build an iron bridge across the Tiber—Lewis's pipes and teacups and beer mugs and hand-annotated editions of the classics fill the display cases of churches and schools across the land and become the subjects of end-less lawsuits, countersuits, and scholarly debates over authenticity?

Such disputes over the Lewisian inheritance are ironic for any num-ber of reasons. If it's odd that America's Protestant evangelicals should start to form at least the external features of a good, old-fashioned Roman Catholic sort of saint's cult, it's even odder that they would choose this Oxford don: those nonsmoking, teetotaling, low-church Americans treasuring the relics of a pipe-smoking, beer-loving, high-church Englishman.

But treasure him they do—and not just evangelicals but serious and religiously conservative Catholics, Eastern Orthodox believers, and mainline Protestants of all stripes. Lewis popularized the term *mere Christianity* to describe basic orthodoxy, the positive faith held by all traditional Christians, whatever their church or sect. And for all those mere Christians Lewis became the author of the twentieth century, by a wide margin the bestselling religious author in England and America.

Beginning in 1996, in anticipation of the centenary of his 1898 birth, dozens of studies of his work were published. For a while almost every time I picked up a Christian magazine or checked my office mail I dis-covered yet another conference devoted to celebrating the anniversary: there were three just at Wheaton College, at least one in every major city in America, and Lord knows how many in England—though the latter set likely was populated chiefly by visiting Americans.

Lewis himself would have been—indeed during his lifetime was—befuddled by this fame. In the early 1950s, after a series of phenome-nally successful BBC radio broadcasts and after his portrait had appeared on the cover of *Time*, he wrote to a friend, "I am going to be (if I live long enough) one of those men who was a famous writer in his forties and dies unknown." Even late in life, when his reputation showed no sign of fading and his books were selling more and more copies, he remained convinced that five years after his death he would no longer be read. And it seems that he really believed this, and didn't mind it: always he attributed his success to the message that he brought, rather than to himself as its messenger, and while not everyone liked Lewis, few who knew him seem to have doubted his sincerity on this point.

He may have been sincere, but he was wrong. And because his popularity shows little sign of fading, it's worthwhile to ask two questions: How are we to account for his enduring fame? And how good a thing is it? Anyone, Christian or not, who wishes to assess the intellectual health of Christianity in the Anglo-American world needs, I believe, to ruminate on these questions. It is not enough to conclude that Lewis is admirable and deserving of our continued attention and honor. Indeed he is, but it remains to discern just what quality of admiration is healthy. The Lewisians' veneration of their hero often fails to do justice to Lewis's legacy and to the Christian cause he served so well.

It's common enough for Americans to refer to Lewis as an Englishman—that's one of the reasons they like him—but in fact he wasn't an Englishman. He was born in Belfast in 1898, was raised as an Ulster Protestant, and came to England for the first time as a schoolboy. Lewis hated school—like many British intellectuals in his century, he found the public school system barbaric—and could thrive only when his father placed him in the hands of a tutor. This memorable character, a Scots Presbyterian turned atheist, prepared Lewis exceedingly well for his Oxford entrance examinations but also solidified the young man in his conviction that religion in any form was something he had to leave behind. After serving in the army in the Great War, Lewis returned to Oxford, took first-class degrees in philosophy and then English, and began a career as a tutor.

Gradually Lewis began to establish himself as a formidable scholar of medieval and Renaissance literature; equally gradually he began to lose his philosophical bearings. In his autobiographical *Surprised by Joy* (1955) he recounts with great verve and wit the collapse of his atheism and his subsequent reluctant conversion, first, in 1929, to theism and then, two years later, to full-fledged Christianity. The latter move was accomplished under the gentle tutelage of two friends, Hugo Dyson of the University of Reading and Lewis's fellow Oxford don J. R. R. Tolkien. Dyson and Tolkien would, some years later, become key members of the amorphous group called the Inklings, who would meet regularly in Lewis's rooms at Magdalen College and at local pubs to drink, smoke, and celebrate poetry—all in a hearty and perhaps excessively masculine atmosphere of "mere Christianity."

In the midst of all these changes Lewis was living a very odd private life. He shared a house with a woman known to history as Mrs. Moore (the mother of an army friend of Lewis who had been killed in the Great War), her daughter, and eventually Lewis's own brother Warnie, a career army officer. Ever since the Lewis cult began there has been speculation about the nature of the relationship with Mrs. Moore: many scholars believe it to have been sexual, but for others (as we shall see) that is an intolerable hypothesis. In any event, Lewis's domestic responsibilities, coupled with his burdens as a popular tutor and lecturer, should have made it impossible for him to get any substantial writing done, but thanks to an astonishing fluency and a stubborn sense of discipline, the works poured from his pen: an allegorical autobiography, *The Pilgrim's Regress* (1933); a profound and still-influential study of medieval poetry, *The Allegory of Love* (1936); a series of science fiction books, beginning with *Out of the Silent Planet* (1938); and, starting with *The Problem of Pain* (1940), a steady stream of works in Christian apologetics that would ultimately make him famous.

These works would also help to make him a much-loathed man in the English faculty of Oxford University. The books were written for a general audience, not a scholarly one, and Lewis made things worse by becoming, during the war, an immensely popular deliverer of radio addresses on the Christian faith. (These would later be printed as *Mere Christianity*.) Moreover, Lewis's characteristic bluffness and heartiness—immensely charming to his friends and most of his students—were no more appealing to many of his colleagues than his Christianity. The result was that Lewis could never get elected to a professorship at Oxford, even though he was by far the most distinguished scholar in the English faculty. So when Cambridge came calling, asking him to stand for a distinguished chair in medieval and Renaissance literature, he ultimately (in 1953) accepted.

Many things were changing in Lewis's life at this time. Mrs. Moore died in 1951. ("And so ends," Lewis's brother Warnie wrote in his diary, "the mysterious self-imposed slavery in which J [for Jack, Lewis's nickname] has lived for at least thirty years.") Lewis had, for reasons that are still debated, stopped writing works of apologetics but had begun a new project: the series of children's books that would become the Chronicles of Narnia and would give him perhaps his greatest and most lasting fame. And he had met Joy Davidman Gresham, who in 1956 became his wife.

The story of their marriage, in its external terms at least, is pretty faithfully told in the film *Shadowlands*. (Most of the complaints Lewisians have made about *Shadowlands* revolve around Anthony Hopkins's portrayal of Lewis as a dour, buttoned-up, somber man—he was anything but—and the film's downplaying of Lewis's Christian faith. These are valid complaints. But there is a vocal minority of Lewisians who argue that the film's portrayal of a sexual relationship between Jack and Joy is unwarranted: they are committed to the belief, for reasons unclear to me, that the marriage remained unconsummated.) The years of marriage to Joy were the most dramatic and emotionally potent, for good and for ill, of Lewis's life, so perhaps it is not surprising that after her death in 1960 his health began to decline. He died on November 22, 1963, but his death did not receive the kind of attention that it might have at another time, for on that same day President John F. Kennedy was shot in Dallas.

So Lewis was not an Englishman, but he was British, and if we wish to inquire into the causes of his lasting popularity, especially in America, that's the best place to begin. Britishness confers for many Americans an immediate air of culture and sophistication—something that American evangelicals have habitually believed themselves to lack. That sophistication is boosted immeasurably by Lewis's status as an Oxford and Cambridge don, for Oxford and Cambridge still dominate their culture in ways no American universities have ever been able to imitate.

But if Americans tend to fawn over certified European cultural sophistication, they dislike what they perceive to be pretension, and here too Lewis fits the bill. Though ideologically he differed greatly from George Orwell, he had Orwell's forcefulness of style—the same relish for slicing through obfuscation, the same let-us-clear-our-minds-of-cant bluntness. Perhaps the most famous example of this sort of thing in Lewis comes in *Mere Christianity*, when he responds to the notion that Jesus was a "great moral teacher":

> A man who was merely a man and said the sort of things Jesus said would not be a great moral teacher. He would either be a lunatic—on a level with the man who says he is a poached egg—or else he would be the Devil of Hell. You must make your choice. Either this man was, and is, the Son of God; or else a madman or something worse. You can shut Him up for a fool, you can spit at Him and kill Him as a demon; or you can fall at his feet and call Him Lord and God. But let us not come with any patronizing nonsense about His being a great human teacher. He has not left that open to us. He did not intend to.

This prose style grows out of a peculiarly English tradition of plain common sense that can be enormously appealing. And the mastery with which Orwell and Lewis employ it is almost sufficient in itself to explain the passion with which each man is admired.

But the style also helps to explain something that is otherwise paradoxical about Lewis's popularity. Living in an age that despised nothing more than moralism, Lewis was a moralist to his bones—perhaps the greatest in the English language since Samuel Johnson. But the candid humility he displayed in even his most polemical writings disarms the usual attacks against moralism. Lewis almost always managed to pass judgment without appearing to be contemptuous or superior: he made it clear that he stood under the same judgment. He wrote clearly, confidently, and unpretentiously because he understood himself to be speaking for a tradition far greater than he. He begins *The Problem of Pain*, for example, by disavowing any deep personal knowledge of pain and fortitude, so that no one could think that his case depended on any virtues of his—though in fact Lewis was, by the time the book was published in 1940, a man well acquainted with suffering. (Even this disavowal, however, did not prevent Lewis's friend Charles Williams from making the deadpan comment that the displeasure God exhibits in the book of Job is directed not to Job so much as to his comforters—"the sort of people who write books on the Problem of Pain.")

Those who enjoy the direct unpretentiousness of his style also tend to be pleased that Lewis was not a professional theologian. Indeed he frequently insisted on his status as an amateur, and though he was deeply learned in the history of Christian theology, the fact that he was not by profession a theologian helped him doubly: it made his strong, plain style all the more appropriate and enabled him to recognize which disputes are too recondite to be of interest to readers with limited theological knowledge.

Moreover, that Lewis was an Anglican, and therefore free to be claimed with almost equal plausibility by people on both sides of that *via media*, helped to minimize denominational bickering—especially in America—and to keep his audience broadly distributed through Christendom. Lewis has been one of the most important figures in modern Christian ecumenism, because, unlike representatives of self-designated ecumenical bodies like the World Council of Churches, he never sought to replace potentially divisive doctrines with supposedly more acceptable commitments—to "Christian Marxism," for instance. For Lewis the demotion of the word *Christian* to a mere adjective was always a bad sign.

This peculiar combination of virtues may have been what led Macmillan—which, until a few years ago, published most of Lewis's best-known books—to splash across the back covers of Lewis's paperbacks the slogan "The Most Original Christian Writer of Our Century." It is a singularly inapt phrase. In the preface to his first volume of Christian apologetics Lewis wrote, "I have believed myself to be re-stating ancient and orthodox doctrines. If any parts of the book are 'original,' in the sense of being novel or unorthodox, they are so against my will and as a result of my ignorance."

If there is anything truly unique about Lewis, it is the facility with which he assimilated influences—and that facility is what gave him both his successes and his failures. The first two volumes of his science fiction trilogy, *Out of the Silent Planet* (1938) and *Perelandra* (1943), were written under the strong influence of David Lindsay's 1920 fantasy, *A Voyage to Arcturus*. But even though some of the characters are carried over to the third volume from the earlier books, *That Hideous Strength* (1945) is wrenchingly different in style and plot—for Lewis had fallen under the spell of Charles Williams's "spiritual thrillers" and saw no difficulty in immediately adopting Williams's peculiar idiom.

Similarly, in his polemical writings Lewis can sometimes sound more Chestertonian than G. K. Chesterton himself. The facility in mimicry has its scholarly uses too: having noted, in his great history of *English Literature in the Sixteenth Century* (1954), that we read older English authors in their own archaic English but translate their Continental counterparts into modern English—a practice that makes the Continental writers sound more like us than the English ones—Lewis proceeds to do all translations in the volume himself and to translate every passage into Renaissance English.

But perhaps the most notable examples of Lewis's ability to assimilate sources is found in his Chronicles of Narnia. In *The Lion, the Witch and the Wardrobe*, for instance, the children speak exactly like children in Edith Nesbit's books; the talking animals come straight out of Kenneth Grahame's *The Wind in the Willows;* the werewolves emerge from the Gothic tradition; and even Father Christmas makes an unexplained appearance. And this is not to mention the gospel story on which the plot is built. Everything in the cupboard goes into the stew.

Lewis's literary acquisitiveness exasperated Tolkien, who believed that the responsibility of the fantasy writer is to build a coherent and internally consistent world. For Tolkien, Lewis's habit of assuming the voices of his favorite writers was both aesthetically and ethically dubious. Nothing infuriated him more than when Lewis used some of Tolkien's terminology—and used it, by Tolkienian standards, inaccurately. Tolkien often said that he could not have finished *The Lord of the Rings* without Lewis's constant support, but he could not return the admiration, and his open frustration with the incoherence of Lewis's fiction played a major part in the cooling of their friendship.

But the trait that Tolkien deplored is also a key to Lewis's success, for it is impossible to find someone left cold by the whole of his work: If not the space trilogy then *The Abolition of Man* is appealing; if not *Reflections on the Psalms* then *Till We Have Faces*. For a writer with Lewis's evangelistic impulses, this ability to exploit a wide range of styles and genres is a wonderful skill to possess. "A young man who wishes to remain a sound Atheist cannot be too careful of his reading," Lewis wrote in his autobiography. "There are traps everywhere. God is, if I may say it, very unscrupulous." Lewis's willingness to appropriate the gifts of his literary forebears was one way he copied the divine unscrupulousness. He was an accomplished literary thief, and nothing in his work is more important to his continuing influence.

If one can, then, understand some of the causes of Lewis's continuing fame, what remains is to consider its value to the Christian faith Lewis stood for. And here the waters are rather muddy. The work of compiling collections of "What Lewis Said About" any number of subjects is virtually complete now, and such work is surely useful, considering the range of topics on which Lewis had valuable thoughts to contribute. But it is hard not to suspect that some people consult these compendia in order to avoid the labor of thinking about difficult subjects themselves. More troublesome still, along these lines, is the new genre devoted to "What Lewis Would Have Said About" problems or issues he did not live long enough to encounter. Perhaps those who expend their ingenuity imagining a Lewisian response to poststructuralism or radical feminism would serve the world and the cause of Christianity better by formulating their own responses to these topics. To be sure, Lewisians at least evidence an admirable willingness to consider that others may be wiser than they. But how many mortals deserve this much reverence? "What would Lewis have said?" is to my mind uncomfortably close to another question—"WWJD," as the bracelets and buttons worn by many young Christians abbreviate it: "What Would Jesus Do?"

Thus the respect readers feel for the man and his work sometimes falls over into idolatry—and with idolatry comes the need to separate the orthodox from the heterodox, the sheep from the goats. More disturbing than the comic disputes over who owns the true wardrobe is the endless disputation about whether Lewis's late-in-life marriage to Joy Davidman Gresham was consummated, with Lewis's literary executor, Walter Hooper, the most vigorous promoter of what A. N. Wilson has wittily called "The Perpetual Virginity of C. S. Lewis." And then there are the fragments of stories and poems that Hooper has published since

Lewis's death, fragments that certain other Lewisians find unworthy of the man (sometimes on stylistic, sometimes on moral, grounds).

Hooper's chief antagonist, Kathryn Lindskoog, has devoted hundreds of pages in books and newsletters to charges that Hooper is a habitual liar and perhaps even complicit in forgery. There are legitimate questions about the way he has handled his exclusive control of the Lewis literary estate, but Hooper has for the most part maintained a lofty silence. And this silence has maddened his critics—especially Lindskoog, who has moved from questioning Hooper's character and motives to questioning those of anyone who doubts her charges.

The whole spectacle is immensely unedifying, and becomes more so when people start to note that Hooper is a late convert to Catholicism who tends to think of Lewis as a kind of crypto-Catholic, while Lindskoog writes for evangelical Protestant publishers. C. S. Lewis's abiding concern was to focus his attention on those foundational beliefs that orthodox Christians have always held in common—beliefs that together constitute *mere Christianity* (a phrase coined by the great seventeenth-century Puritan Richard Baxter). Lewis contends that this "plain, central" Christian faith, when examined closely and historically, "turns out to be no insipid interdenominational transparency, but something positive, self-consistent, and inexhaustible." Because it is positive, it provides direction for the spiritual inquirer; because it is self-consistent, it provides security; because it is inexhaustible, it provides delight.

Perhaps this delightful inexhaustibility is also Lewis's most noteworthy trait: he saw himself as simply the most recent in a long series of writers who have tried over the centuries to restate the essentials of the Christian faith for their time. That is why he did not think his books would be read for long after his death: he expected that history would present new challenges for the Christian church, which new generations of Christian writers would have to address in their own way, not by reinventing Christian doctrine but by creatively re-presenting that same plain, central, inexhaustible Christianity to which he devoted his ability, energy, and delight.

We should therefore ask whether those Christians who honored Lewis in his centenary year—and it was fitting so to honor him—always did so in the best way. Many years ago V. S. Naipaul noted a peculiarity of the Indian attitude toward Gandhi: everywhere in India Gandhi was venerated as a saint, but the social conditions against which he railed for so long remained unchanged. It would be sad if the same fate were to befall Lewis, if people were to revere his achievement so much that they fail to devote the quality of attention to the challenges of their time that he devoted to the challenges of his. This is a real temptation for those of us who love Lewis, because to read his books is to dwell in an atmosphere of moral and spiritual health that offers dramatic relief from the confusions and frustrations, petty and grand, of modern life. But Lewis himself always strove to encounter and interpret the world in which he lived. His admirers should remember that the achievements of the truly great are best honored not by the one who praises their work but by the one who follows their example.

11

DONALD DAVIE

IN THE SUMMER OF 1994 I found myself in a train heading west across England toward the city of Exeter. From there I would travel to a village set among low green hills to visit Donald Davie. As I rode I thumbed through a paperback copy of *The Tempest*, which I was scheduled to teach the next day, and since Donald had said not long before that he would write no more poetry, my eyes were naturally drawn to Prospero's famous repudiation of his magical arts, a speech long taken to refer to Shakespeare's plans to retire from *his* poetry.

> But this rough magic
> I here abjure; and when I have requir'd
> Some heavenly music (which even now I do)
> To work mine end upon their senses that
> This airy charm is for, I'll break my staff,
> Bury it certain fathoms in the earth,
> And deeper than did ever plummet sound
> I'll drown my book.

As I turned to watch the town of Swindon pass dully by my window, it occurred to me that my implicit comparison of Donald and Prospero was a singularly inapt one. No one would have been quicker than Donald to repudiate any attempt to make poetry into a form of magic. In this, as in most things of import, his career from its inception was of one piece.

I did not know Donald nearly as well as I would have liked. He came to my school, fifteen years ago now, to deliver a lecture on the chief theme of his later critical career, the poetic excellence of the eighteenth-century hymnists: Cowper, Smart, and especially Watts. (Later he would tell me that Watts "has been for many years now in many respects my hero.") He stood at the lectern, a solidly built man of middle height and firm (not to say forbidding) countenance. He was sixty-two then: his dark hair was streaked with gray, chiefly at the temples, and he was developing the jowls of the older man. These developments helped to make him look puckish at times—perhaps they softened the primness I think I see around his mouth when I look at earlier pictures. He rarely looked at his audience as he spoke, but occasionally peered at us over the spectacles that had slid down his nose, as though merely to confirm our continued presence.

Donald found it necessary to illustrate his lecture by ample, if well-chosen, selections from the relevant poems, and as a result considerably overran his time limit. This is scarcely uncommon at an academic lecture, but the next-scheduled occupants of the room were less than patient, and one of them interrupted Donald in midsentence. His eyes lifted from his text and, from under his formidable Vaughan Williams eyebrows, fixed the intruder with a scornful look that after a moment metamorphosed into a sardonic smile. As he tucked his notes under his arm and marched out of the room, a resourceful person grabbed a folding chair and suggested that Donald take a seat under a nearby oak tree—it was a lovely early-autumn day—to complete his lecture. Only when he realized that this would enable him to light his pipe (in the lecture hall smoking had been prohibited) did Donald accept the offer, and as twenty or thirty people arranged themselves on the grass around him like the eager pupils of Socrates, what had been a conventional lecture became a charmingly digressive monologue. Donald sat with legs crossed, a length of white English calf showing between trouser cuff and sock, and gestured with his pipe in the mottled shade of the oak. He was starting to enjoy himself.

It was while he was in this mood that I met him, and as we walked across campus talking about poetry I wondered if he would be receptive to a continuation of our conversation, if merely by letter. He was, though only intermittently until he retired from Vanderbilt University and returned full time to the Devonshire village where for many years he had spent his summers. Our correspondence increased dramatically then: "Here, in my retirement," he wrote, "I'm particularly dependent on letters from my friends." This isolation was intensified by the increasing unreliability of his legs—he was beginning to take the occasional but frightening fall—but also by what he called his "physical indolence": "I take retirement seriously, in a way that puzzles others, including my wife. I mean that I seldom find reasons for leaving this village." So I had to come to Donald if I wished to see him, and that, in the summer of '94, is what I was finally able to do.

As I rode toward Exeter I asked myself whether it was not presumptuous of me to visit. Donald had been encouraging, but I knew that the differences in our cultures and our ages (he was thirty-five years my senior) limited our relationship in important ways. Still, there was a bond. We were both Christians and lovers of poetry—categories that do not regularly overlap; we were both moralists by temperament and practice; perhaps most important of all, we were people from similarly marginal regions of our native countries. He was a Baptist-turned-Anglican from northern industrial England, I a Baptist-turned-Anglican from Alabama. He had lived in the American South long enough (while teaching at Vanderbilt) to appreciate the ways it was like the world in which he was reared.

But even these links don't bear much emphasis: to be a Baptist in Alabama is a very different thing than to be a Baptist in England, and the Alabama Baptist who joins the Anglican communion sends a very different cultural message than the Yorkshire Baptist who joins the Anglican communion. As for the time Donald spent in Tennessee, he described himself as only a "bemused but attracted Southerner-by-courtesy." Above all I had no access to his deep and persistent sense of being a Northerner (the North being for Donald "the region of the stripped and the straitened, the necessitous")—and a Northerner from a country whose center of gravity is notably low. This feeling of detachment from what conventional wisdom deems the heart of things was dear to him, in his retirement as in his childhood.

Donald was ever the contrarian. He was far more likely, when referring to his religious upbringing, to call himself a dissenter than a Baptist—though this may have been, in part, a concession to the Anglican
establishment's lack of interest in the varieties of dissent. And contrarian from an early age, not just because he was "Chapel" rather than
"Church"—in northern England that was scarcely uncommon—but
also because his family always voted Tory, "though without hope," in
a Labour stronghold. (I'm quoting in this paragraph from his memoir
These the Companions.) At Cambridge he was "happy" to join the
Robert Hall Society, an association of Cambridge's Baptists, even
though his attachment to his Baptist roots had become tenuous, not
to say indiscernible. He seems to have become comfortable in the
Anglican tradition only in places where it was *not* the established communion. This first happened during his years teaching at Trinity College, Dublin, where "the disestablished Church of Ireland satisfied the
need, bred in me as a child, to envisage my church as in tension with
the state." Later, when he had moved to California to teach at Stan-
ford—after the most frustrating time of his academic life, a period in
the early 1960s when he sought with limited success to establish an
academically rigorous English curriculum at the new University of
Essex—Donald found an Episcopalian priest whom he described as
his "mentor," a word he used elsewhere only in reference to his greatest critical influences, the Englishman F. R. Leavis and the American
Ivor Winters.

This contrarian temperament can be seen equally clearly in Donald's poetry and his criticism. In a time when the most influential
British poets posited a Romantic or an Augustan aesthetic (see Dylan
Thomas and W. H. Auden, respectively), Donald sought out the poets
of the late eighteenth century and claimed them as his masters. It was
the poets in between, like Cowper and Goldsmith and (a rather later
figure) Crabbe, whom he most admired. Later on, as I have noted, he
would become the champion of Isaac Watts and would fill his poems
with echoes of Watts's hymns. Donald's poetry can be analytical and
dry, knotty, concerned with geography and history in ways one might
expect more from an essayist. (One of Donald's longest poems con-

cerns the English sailor James Trevenen, who shared with Crabbe the patronage of Edmund Burke. Who else would have devoted five hundred lines to such a figure?) Early on he named his poetic gift a "winter talent"; he would return much later to that self-descriptive image. His criticism, on the other hand, is never disinterested but rather heated, passionate, and moralizing. It is utterly characteristic of Donald that in his first book of criticism one of the key terms he employs to describe verse of which he approves is *chastity*. Once when I asked him why he had written so little on Auden, whom I thought would be a very sympathetic figure for him, he agreed that he admired Auden enormously, but explained that he had had little to say about him because, as he put it, "I never thought Auden needed any help from me." Since judicious assessment revealed that Auden's reputation was neither inflated nor deflated, Donald chose to devote his critical energies to figures whom he thought had been neglected (the aforementioned hymnists) or misunderstood (Ezra Pound). Auden needed no critical knight to come to his rescue.

If the analytical tension of Donald's verse brought it to the verge of essayistic reflection and criticism, the sheer and unapologetic partisanship of his criticism brought *it* to the verge of poetry. And indeed, when in 1992 Donald looked back at his early writings, he reflected on just this point: "The critic . . . has to be—so it is assumed—clinical, detached, Olympian. . . . [But] the young man who wrote these essays was the same who, in poems of the same time, was wrestling the actualities of Plymouth and Dublin into a significance that satisfied him. For him then, as for me now rereading him, essay and poem were equivalent and almost interchangeable attempts to grapple with the one same reality." But this grappling often seemed, at least, to be more intense in Donald's criticism. To the end of his life Donald seemed to be aroused to the greatest passion by arguments over even the smallest detail of criticism or historical scholarship; a memorable instance for me is his acrimonious dispute, conducted with another scholar in the correspondence pages of the *London Review of Books*, about the identity of the man wearing blood-covered garments in the sixty-third chapter of Isaiah.

Donald's long-term fascination with Pound—about whom he wrote a monograph and a substantial book of essays—is a wonderful illustration of his dissenting spirit, because there is no figure in modern poetry with whom one would expect Donald to be less sympathetic. After all, Donald's lifelong devotion to traditional poetic forms, his tendency to confine himself to shorter poems, and his general conservatism and traditionalism would all seem to bear little affinity with the rebellious and flamboyant American who sought to "break the pentameter." And indeed I suspect that Donald would have had little patience with any British poet who tried to write like Pound. But Donald believed that the idioms in which Pound worked were often appropriate not only for a poet of Pound's nationality but also for one of his historical situation— often appropriate, but not always: "I have as often been exasperated by Pound as exalted and delighted by him." But this exasperation was not necessarily something to lament: "A love affair comprehends exasperation along with exaltation." In passages such as this one sees that Donald's contrarian temperament was no mere curmudgeonliness but arose from a sense of gratitude to gadflies like Pound, who are among the more socially useful animals.[2] And Pound may have been no more distant from his culture's center than Donald was from his.

But though Donald relished the gadfly's vocation, he understood perfectly well that (like all vocations) it carries accompanying spiritual dangers. One of the poems from his troubled Essex period, "Revulsion," is a severe self-analysis in which the jeremiad—which Donald admitted was the literary genre that he most naturally assumed—verges on lament:

>My strongest feeling all
>My life has been,
>I recognize, revulsion
>From the obscene;

2. Donald's concern with Pound is but part of his larger and still more long-standing interest in American culture: starting with the lengthy "Sequence for Francis Parkman" in 1961, and continuing through the last section in his *Collected Poems*, "Goodbye to the USA," Donald would return again and again to reflection upon the people, the history, and the geography of North America. A noteworthy theme in his work is the Englishman abroad, especially on this continent; among his longest individual poems are extended treatments of the English sailors and navigators James Trevenen and George Vancouver.

>   That more than anything
>   My life-consuming passion.
>
>   That so much more reaction
>   Than action should have swayed
>   My life and rhymes
>   Must be the heaviest charge
>   That can be brought against
>   Me, or my times.

Those last three words alter the balance of the poem in interesting ways: from self-critique emerges at least the possibility of cultural critique. (Who is to blame for the failures of this new university?) A less ambiguous self-indictment comes a decade later in "St Paul's Revisited," the second of "Depravity: Two Sermons" (a title stolen from Auden). Here Donald teases out some of the subtle discriminations to be made among terms that for most people are synonyms: *anger, ire, rancor*. And this poem I understand the better because of another notable and notably anti-Prosperan trait of Donald's, his willingness to explain his poems to the honestly confused.

I had made the mistake of telling Donald that he was often a difficult poet, and compounded this error with the still grosser one of comparing him in this respect to Geoffrey Hill. Now, my recollection is that I meant to contrast the *difficulty* of Donald's poetry with the *obscurity* of Hill's, but Donald failed to admire that distinction as I had hoped he would, and indeed became indignant at the very thought of being linked with Geoffrey Hill (in this respect anyway). "I will not accept that my poetry is as difficult as Geoffrey Hill's!" Donald wrote to me, refuting an imaginary claim, and then continued:

> Regarding the second of my "Depravity: Two Sermons," the word "Revisited" in my title "St Paul's Revisited" is meant I'm afraid to refer back to my "Under St Paul's" [a poem from his second collection, *A Winter Talent*, from 1957]. In that earlier poem I tend to identify with "gulls," taken to stand for Anger, confronted with London's depravity. Twenty years later I find that response too self-comforting: not only is Anger (Ire) itself a sin, but I convict myself of not Anger but Rancour (not the white gull but the multicoloured hoopoe); and depravity is located not in the "out there" (contemporary London) but

in the head (or the heart) of the too easily indignant patriot. I take the point that you don't want this or any poem to be exhaustively explainable: I give you only what I consciously put there—there's a penumbra of other meanings that are doubtless there, beyond my intentions. But I'd feel ashamed if I couldn't, when challenged, come up with that much of an explanation. I guess that Hill couldn't, or wouldn't. Accordingly, when or if you care to face me with other "difficulties," I'd be glad to oblige.

The quotation marks around "difficulties" in the last sentence is a characteristic touch, a nip at the ankle of the overbold stranger who is no doubt already making tracks. But more important is Donald's insistence that he would be "ashamed" if he "couldn't, or wouldn't" offer precisely the sort of explanatory gloss on his verse that not only Hill but most contemporary poets would consider it near-heresy to provide, as if he would take any opportunity to puncture the Prosperan view of poetry as inexplicable magic.

Indeed in many cases Donald didn't even wait to be asked for an explanation. Fairly early in our correspondence he expressed his pleasure at my having noted that his last book of poems, *To Scorch or Freeze*, which is filled with paraphrases of or responses to the Psalms, is in the dithyrambic tradition whose greatest modern practitioner (as Donald himself argued) is Czeslaw Milosz. And having thanked me, he went on:

> Because you have been so kind towards *To Scorch or Freeze*, I think I will show off a little. Take my poem, "Except the Lord Build the House." This title plainly signposts the reader to Psalm 127 in the King James version.... However, "Short be your sleep and coarse your fare" is a straight steal from Watts's version of this Psalm; and "No use of early rising;/ as useless is thy watching" comes from the Elizabethan Sidney Psalter. Lines 6 through 8 come from another psalm (122, v. 3), and later lines draw on yet another, Psalm 129, as rendered admirably by Watts. Moreover the same verses, as rendered by the Calvinist Arthur Golding in 1571, give me "no one/ going by in the road calls out/ 'Good morning' or 'Good luck.'" Thus [Mikhail] Bakhtin's plurality of voices is built into these poems to a degree that no one will, or is expected to, notice. Add that "Eblis" comes from Pound (Canto 27 and elsewhere), and it will appear how far I am from "the traditional monologue of the lyrist."

(If the quotation marks around "difficulties" in the previously cited letter was a neat example of Daviean acerbity, here the parenthetical "or is expected to" marks an equally common kindness.) Whatever Donald may have said of the isolation of his little Devonshire village, in letters like this I hear a poet surrounded by the voices of fellow poets, finding with them a fellowship composed equally of the love of verse and a deep attachment to the Christian faith.

Donald rarely wrote directly about his spiritual life; in this he followed (as he was quick to say) the British rather than the American fashion. But I believe his faith became more important to him as he grew older. One sees this not only in the way he chose to end his poetic career, with the psalmic variations of *To Scorch or Freeze*, but also in his celebration of Watts and in his last major critical and editorial projects: a book on the eighteenth-century congregational hymn, an anthology of translations of the Psalms. It sometimes seemed, in the last years of Donald's life, that his faith had become a kind of balm to his combativeness, especially since so many of the causes he fought for lost ground quite steadily despite the eloquence of his support. (Again the Essex experience comes to mind.)

Once, in what he called "a rather arid letter," he expressed frustration at how quickly even the best and most cogent critical work can be forgotten, thanks to the academy's lust for sheer novelty. In such a climate, he said, he scarcely lacked "things to say" but couldn't "envisage circumstances in which saying them would have much point." At times Donald considered the possibility that his lapsing into silence could be an intellectual version of the "physical indolence" to which, as I have noted, he was quick to plead guilty. In a late poem he reflects on a poetic "dry season" and notes with mild surprise, first, that "the nice distinction / Of colon from semi-colon / That once absorbed" him now bores him, and, second, that he does not mind his own loss of interest.

> Sloth; why is it always
> Spoken of so ill?
>
> It does no harm; it spares
> The inattentive world

> One more triumphant play
> Out of my one strong suit,
> Sardonic paradox:
> This age's mask for love.

(Need I point out, however, that this very poem demonstrates an undiminished ability to use both colon and semicolon effectively and with nuance?) In such a mood he took comfort in his sense of God as what Mikhail Bakhtin would call the "superaddressee" of his work: "We can tell God in our prayers that what we write is meant to His Glory; that is the one and only justification that we have."

I was glad that Donald could summon such comfort; but it seemed to be rather cold, or "arid," comfort, and uneasily I considered one of the poems in *To Scorch or Freeze*, "Inditing a Good Matter." This poem cites the beginning of Psalm 45, "My heart is inditing a good matter." but in another tense: "My heart had been inditing / a good matter." Now, the poet admits,

> I find nothing to say,
> I am heavy as lead.
> I take small satisfaction
> in anything I have said. . . .

> [God] shrugs. How can He care
> what *billets-doux* we send Him,
> how much we applaud? Such coxcombs
> inclined to commend Him!

Given the strength—and not just for Donald—of this darker, if equally biblical and traditional, valuation of Christian writing, I was rather trepid when, a few months later, I paid the visit that I referred to at the beginning of this essay. And of course my train-bound reflections on Prospero's abjuration didn't help, however firmly (and rightly) did I deem them inappropriate.

But the Donald I found that day was vigorous and talkative, anything but arid. He was grayer and heavier than he had been ten years before, but otherwise much the same: the same ironic look from under the brows, the same use of the pipe—whether smoking, filling, or tapping it—for conversational punctuation. There were anecdotes about his fellow critics and poets, revelations of new scholarly discoveries, a repeated if fruitless search for recordings of some favorite hymns. After having announced to me that he could no longer ambulate without his cane, he left it leaning against something half a dozen times and had to retrace his steps to find it. At one point he dug through a pile of magazines to find the issues of the *London Review of Books* in which his row about Isaiah's blood-covered man had been conducted, and read his side of the exchange to me with the oratorical verve of a Dylan Thomas and a good deal of unsuccessfully suppressed laughter.

When he and his wife, Doreen, dropped me at the Exeter railway station that evening, Doreen whispered to me that the visit had done Donald good; but I think it did me much more good. As the train took me back toward Oxford I sat looking through a pile of books Donald had given me—those of his books I did not already have—and considered the example of intellectual courage and integrity they represented. I did not see him again.

For Donald the writing of poetry, like the writing of criticism, wasn't magic; like Auden he loathed Shelley's claim that "poets are the unacknowledged legislators of the world." No, it was a way of engaging an old and rich conversation. And of course for the real lover of conversation, argument—even when it crosses the borderline into the territory of polemic or jeremiad, even when it risks ire and rancour—is the supreme spice. Donald believed that the value of discussion depends upon its heatedness, its heatedness upon the importance of the subject. He cared about poetry, about criticism, about Isaiah's blood-covered man, because he believed that the decisions one makes about such matters determine—in small or large part, one can never be sure—the value of mortal life.

For Donald—and this distinguishes him from many contemporary proponents of "dialogue"—conversation is never an end in itself; it matters only insofar as it dispels darkness or encourages virtue. This conviction alone is sufficient to earn Donald Davie our attention, and after that our gratitude.

12

HARRY POTTER'S
MAGIC

BY NOW MOST AMERICAN readers are aware of what has come to be called the Harry Potter phenomenon. It's hard to be unaware. Any bookstore you might care to enter is strewn with giant stacks of the Harry Potter books—four of them now that *Harry Potter and the Goblet of Fire* has finally been released. This blessed event, concurrent in the United States and Britain, comes after some years during which, thanks to American versions appearing some months after their British counterparts, the online bookstore Amazon.co.uk devoted much of its energy to shipping copies across the Atlantic. This created a miniature trade war, as lawyers on both sides of the pond tried to figure out which country a book is purchased in when it's ordered *from* a British company but *on* a computer in America. Whatever the legal status of cyberspatial commerce, anyone visiting either Amazon.com or Amazon.co.uk last summer could not but note that the bestselling books on both sites were the Harry Potter novels, which ranked a consistent one, two, and three.

Many people are also familiar with the story behind the most talked-about children's books in decades, perhaps ever: how Joanne Rowling, an out-of-work teacher and single mother living on the dole in Edinburgh, started scribbling a story in a local café as her small daughter dozed in a stroller; how an English publisher, Bloomsbury Books, took a chance on this unknown author; and how, almost wholly by word-of-mouth reports, the first novel, *Harry Potter and the Philosopher's Stone*, became a bestseller not just among children but also among adults, for whom Bloomsbury designed a more mature-looking cover so commuters on bus and tube would not have to be embarrassed as they eagerly followed Harry's quest to discover what the enormous three-headed dog, Fluffy, was guarding in that off-limits corridor of Hogwarts School of Witchcraft and Wizardry. International success, as indicated by those great piles of books at 40 percent discount and the dominance of Amazon's bestseller lists, quickly followed.

In the twentysome-odd years that I have been pretty closely following trends in American publishing, no development in the industry has been so nearly inexplicable to me, nor has any development made me so happy, for I adore the Harry Potter books. I read the first one—under its silly American title, *Harry Potter and the Sorcerer's Stone* (the American publisher evidently judged that no book with the word *philosopher* in it could sell)—thinking that it might be something I could read to my son. Though I decided that he wasn't quite old enough, at six, to follow the rather complicated plot, I was hooked, and in my impatience I ordered each of the next two novels in the series from Amazon.co.uk, thus making my own personal contribution to the perplexity of international trade law. (The remaining books in the series—Rowling plans a total of seven—will be published simultaneously in the U.S. and the U.K., thus cutting the legal Gordian knot.)

J. K. Rowling, as the books' covers have it—the name rhymes with "bowling"—simply has that mysterious gift, so prized among storytellers and lovers of stories but so resistant to critical explication, of world-making. It is a gift that many Christian readers tend to associate with that familiar but rather amorphous group of English Christian writers, the Inklings—though the association is not quite proper, because only one of the Inklings, J. R. R. Tolkien, had this rare faculty and few of the others even aspired to it. Tolkien, however, possessed the power in spades and gave useful names to its elements as well: he spoke of the "secondary worlds" created by the writer and of "mythopoeia" as the activity of such "sub-creation." The *sine qua non* of such mythopoeia, for Tolkien, is the making of a world that resembles ours but is not ours, a world that possesses internal logic and self-consistency to the same degree that ours does—but not the same logic. It must have its own rules, rules that are peculiar to it and that generate consequences also peculiar to it.

It is important to understand that C. S. Lewis's Narnia books, great though they may be, are not in this strict sense mythopoeic. Lewis does not want to create a self-consistent secondary world but rather a world in which all the varieties of mythology meet and find their home. In Narnia there is no internal consistency whatever, thus Father Christmas can show up in the middle of *The Lion, the Witch and the Wardrobe* and Bacchus and Silenus in the middle of *Prince Caspian*. It may well be that this mythographic promiscuity, so to speak, is key to the success of the Chronicles of Narnia, but it makes them very different books from Tolkien's, and it is the reason Tolkien hated the Narnia stories. They lacked the clearly demarcated wholeness that he considered the essential virtue of his own Middle Earth.

Joanne Rowling has expressed her love for the Narnia books—one of the reasons there will be, God willing, seven Harry Potter books is that there are seven volumes of Narnia stories—but as a literary artist she bears a far greater resemblance to Tolkien. One of the great pleasures for the reader of her books is the wealth of details, from large to small, that mark the magic world as different from ours (which in the books is called the Muggle world): the tall pointed hats the students wear in their classes, in which they study such topics as Potions, Transfiguration, Defense Against the Dark Arts, and even Care of Magical Creatures; the spells that are always in Latin (*"Expelliarmus!"*); or the universal addiction to Quidditch, a game that shares some characteristics with basketball, cricket, and soccer but is played in the air, on broomsticks, and with four balls. Rowling's attention to such matters is remarkable and charming, especially when the details are small: once when Harry is visiting the home of a friend from a magical family, he steps over a pack of self-shuffling playing cards. It's an item that could have been left out without any loss to the narrative, but it offers an elegant little surprise—and another piece of furniture for this thoroughly imagined universe.

I have made my enthusiasm for these books quite evident to many friends, but some of them are dubious—indeed deeply suspicious. These are Christian people, and they feel that books that make magic so funny and charming don't exactly support the Christian view of things: such novels could at best encourage children to take a smilingly tolerant New Age view of witchcraft, at worst encourage the practice of witchcraft itself. Moreover, some of them note, Harry Potter is not exactly a model student. He has, as the headmaster of Hogwarts puts it, "a certain disregard for rules" and spends a good deal of time fervently hoping not to get caught in mid-disregard.

This second matter, I think, poses no real problem. It is true that Harry is often at odds with some of his teachers, but these particular teachers are not exactly admirable figures. They themselves are often at odds with the wise, benevolent, and powerful headmaster, Albus Dumbledore, whom they sometimes attempt to undermine or outflank. But to Dumbledore, significantly, Harry is unswervingly faithful and obedient; indeed, the climax of the second novel, *Harry Potter and the Chamber of Secrets,* turns on Harry's fidelity to Dumbledore. Moreover, Harry's tendency to bypass or simply flout the rules is a matter of moral concern for him. He wonders and worries about the self-justifications he offers, and often doubts not just his abilities but his virtue. He is constantly aware that his great unchosen antagonist, Voldemort—the Dark Lord, the most evil of wizards and, after Dumbledore, the most powerful—offers temptations to which he cannot simply assume that he is immune. And when Dumbledore mentions Harry's "certain disregard for rules" he does so in a way that links such disregard with the forces of evil, thus warning Harry (though his larger purpose in that scene is to encourage the troubled young wizard).

In short, Rowling's moral compass throughout the three novels is sound—I would even say acute. But the matter of witchcraft remains, and it is not a matter to be trifled with. People today, and this includes many Christians, tend to hold two views about witches: first, that real witches don't exist, and second, that they aren't as bad as the evil masterminds of the Salem witch trials made them out to be. These are obviously incompatible beliefs. As Lewis has pointed out, there is no virtue in being tolerant of witches if you think that witchcraft is impossible, that is, that witches don't really exist. But if there are such things as witches, and they do indeed invoke supernatural or unnatural forces to bring harm to good people, then it would be neither wise nor good to tolerate them. So the issue is an important one and worthy of serious reflection. (Incidentally, Rowling has flatly said, in response to questions about whether her books might prompt children to pursue witchcraft, that she doesn't believe in magic.)

It is tempting to say, in response to these concerns, that Harry Potter is not that kind of wizard, that he doesn't do harm to anyone except those who are manifestly evil and trying to do harm to him, or that no one, in Harry's world, can become a wizard by wanting to—it's not a career choice. And these are significant points. But an answer to our question must begin elsewhere.

The place to begin is to invoke one of the great achievements of twentieth-century historical scholarship: the eight volumes Lynn Thorndike published between 1929 and 1941 under the collective title *A History of Magic and Experimental Science*, and it is primarily the title that I wish to reflect upon here. In the thinking of most modern people there should be two histories here. After all, are not magic and experimental science opposites? Is not magic governed by superstition, ignorance, and wishful thinking, while experimental science is rigorous, self-critical, and methodological? While the two paths have indeed diverged to the point that they no longer have any point of contact, for much of their existence—and this is Thorndike's chief point—they constituted a single path with a single history, for both magic and experimental science are means of controlling and directing our natural environment (and people, insofar as they are part of that environment). Lewis has made the same assertion:

[Francis Bacon's] endeavour is no doubt contrasted in our minds with that of the magicians: but contrasted only in the light of the event, only because we know that science succeeded and magic failed. That event was then still uncertain. Stripping off our knowledge of it, we see at once that Bacon and

the magicians have the closest possible affinity. . . . Nor would Bacon himself
deny the affinity: he thought the aim of the magicians was "noble."

It was not obvious in advance that science would succeed and magic
fail. In fact, several centuries of dedicated scientific experiment would
have to pass before it was clear to anyone that the "scientific" physician could do more to cure illness than the old woman of the village
with her herbs and potions and muttered charms. Similarly, in the
Renaissance alchemists were divided between those who sought to
solve problems—the achievement of the philosopher's stone, for example (or should I say the sorcerer's stone?)—primarily through the use
of what we would call mixtures of chemicals and those who relied more
heavily on incantations, the drawing of mystical patterns, and the invo-
cation of spirits. At least it seems to us that the alchemists can be so
divided, but that's because we know that one approach developed into
chemistry while the other became pure magic. The division may not
have been nearly so evident at the time, when (to adapt Weber's famous
phrase) the world had not yet become disenchanted. As Keith Thomas
has shown, it was "the triumph of the mechanical philosophy" of nature
that "meant the end of the animistic conception of the universe which
had constituted the basic rationale for magical thinking." Even after the
powerful work of mechanistic scientists like Gassendi the change was
not easily completed. Isaac Newton, whose name is associated more
than any other with physical mechanics, was continually absorbed by
alchemical research, as John Maynard Keynes, the famous economist,
learned when, in 1936, he bought Newton's alchemical manuscripts at
auction. A stunned Keynes wrote a paper in which he revealed that Newton, far from being "the first and greatest . . . rationalist," was instead
"the last of the magicians."

   This history provides a key to understanding the role of magic in
Joanne Rowling's books, for she begins by positing a counterfactual
history, a history in which magic was not a false and incompetent discipline but rather a means of controlling the physical world at least as
potent as experimental science. In Harry Potter's world, scientists think
of magic in precisely the same way they do in our world, but they are

wrong. The counterfactual "secondary world" that Rowling creates is one in which magic simply works, and works as reliably, in the hands of a trained wizard, as the technology that makes airplanes fly and refrigerators chill the air—those products of applied science being, by the way, sufficiently inscrutable to the people who use them that they might as well be the products of wizardry. As Arthur C. Clarke once wrote, "Any smoothly functioning technology gives the appearance of magic."

The fundamental moral framework of the Harry Potter books, then, is a familiar one to all of us: it is the problem of technology. (Jacques Ellul has speculated that "magic may even be the origin of techniques.") Hogwarts School of Witchcraft and Wizardry is in the business of teaching people how to harness and employ certain powers—that they are powers unrecognized by science is really beside the point. But the school cannot ensure that people will use those powers wisely, responsibly, and for the common good. It is a choice, as the thinkers of the Renaissance would have put it, between *magia* and *goetia*, between "high magic" (like the wisdom possessed by the magi in Christian legend) and "dark magic." Hogwarts was founded by four wizards, one of whom, Salazar Slytherin, at least dabbled and perhaps reveled in the Dark Arts, that is, in the use of his powers for questionable if not downright evil purposes, and for centuries many of the young wizards who have resided in Slytherin House have exhibited the same tendency. The educational quandary for Albus Dumbledore, then—though it is never described so overtly—is how to train students not just in the "technology" of magic but also in the moral discernment necessary to avoid the continual reproduction of the few great dark lords like Voldemort and their multitudinous followers. The problem is exacerbated by the presence of faculty members who are not wholly unsympathetic with Voldemort's aims.

The clarity with which Rowling sees the need to choose between good and evil is admirable, but still more admirable, to my mind, is her refusal to allow a simple division of parties into the good and the evil. Harry Potter is unquestionably a good (though by no means perfect) boy, but as I have suggested, much of his virtue arises from his recognition that he is not *inevitably* good. When first-year students arrive at Hogwarts, they come to an assembly of the entire school, both students and faculty. Each first-year student sits on a stool in the midst of the assembly and puts on a large, battered old hat—the Sorting Hat—which decides which of the four houses the student will enter. After unusually long reflection, the Sorting Hat, to Harry's great relief, puts him in Gryffindor, but not before telling him that he could achieve real greatness in Slytherin. This comment haunts Harry; he often wonders whether Slytherin is where he truly belongs, among the pragmatists, the careerists, the manipulators and deceivers, the power-hungry, and the just plain nasty.

Near the end of the second book, after a terrifying encounter with Voldemort—his third: Voldemort had tried to kill Harry, and succeeded in killing his parents, when Harry was a baby, and Voldemort had confronted Harry again in the first book—Harry confesses his doubts to Dumbledore.

> "So I should be in Slytherin," Harry said, looking desperately into Dumbledore's face. "The Sorting Hat could see Slytherin's power in me, and it—"
>
> "Put you in Gryffindor," said Dumbledore calmly. "Listen to me, Harry. You happen to have many qualities Salazar Slytherin prized in his hand-picked students. . . . Resourcefulness . . . determination . . . a certain disregard for rules," he added, his moustache quivering again. "Yet the Sorting Hat placed you in Gryffindor. You know why that was. Think."
>
> "It only put me in Gryffindor," said Harry in a defeated voice, "because I asked not to go in Slytherin . . ."
>
> "Exactly," said Dumbledore, beaming once more. "Which makes you very different from [Voldemort]. It is our choices, Harry, that show what we truly are, far more than our abilities." Harry sat motionless in his chair, stunned.

Harry is stunned because he realizes for the first time that his confusion has been wrong-headed from the start. He has been asking the question "Who am I at heart?" when he needed to be asking the question "What must I do in order to become what I should be?" His character is not a fixed, preexistent thing, but something he has responsibility for making; that's why the Greeks called it character, "that which is engraved"—the metal is capable of receiving and retaining a distinctive impression, but the impression once made is hard to erase.[3] It's also what the Germans mean when they speak of *Bildung*, and the Harry Potter books are of course a multivolume *Bildungsroman*—a story of education, that is to say, of character formation.

In this sense the strong tendency of magic to become a dream of power—on the importance of this point Lynn Thorndike, Keith Thomas, and C. S. Lewis all agree—makes it a wonderful means by which to focus the theme of *Bildung*, of the choices that gradually but inexorably shape us into certain distinct kinds of persons. Christians are perhaps right to be wary of an overly positive portrayal of magic, but the Harry Potter books don't do that: in them magic is often fun, often surprising and exciting, but also always potentially dangerous.

And so, it should be said, is technology that has resulted from the victory of experimental science. Perhaps the most important question I could ask my Christian friends who mistrust the Harry Potter books

---

3. However, the annual ritual of the Sorting Hat suggests that by the time they enter Hogwarts, at age eleven or so, the children have already had their characters formed to a considerable extent. The ritual always commences with a song from the hat: "'Sings a different one every year,' said [Harry's friend] Ron. 'It's got to be a pretty boring life, hasn't it, being a hat? I suppose it spends all year making up the next one.'" In *The Goblet of Fire* here's part of what the hat sings:

> Now each of these four founders
> Formed their own house, for each
> Did value different virtues
> In the ones they had to teach.
> By Gryffindor, the bravest were
> Prized far beyond the rest;
> For Ravenclaw, the cleverest
> Would always be the best;
> For Hufflepuff, hard workers were
> Most worthy of admission;
> And power-hungry Slytherin
> Loved those of great ambition. . . .
> Now slip me snug about your ears,
> I've never yet been wrong,
> I'll have a look inside your mind
> And tell where you belong!

In the four books to appear so far, no one has gone clearly against the ethos of his or her House. I would like to see that change.

is this: Is your concern about the portrayal of this imaginary magical technology matched by a concern for the effects of the technology that in our world displaced magic? The technocrats of this world hold in their hands powers almost infinitely greater than those of Albus Dumbledore and Voldemort. How worried are we about them, and about their influence over our children? Not worried enough, I would say. As Ellul suggests, the task for us is "the measuring of technique by other criteria than those of technique itself," which measuring he also calls "the search for justice before God." Joanne Rowling's books are more helpful than most in prompting such measurement. They are also— and let's not forget the importance of this point—a great deal of fun.

13

BLINDED
BY THE LIGHT

I TAKE AS MY TEXT THE WORDS of a little girl who once spoke with Melvin
Morse, a doctor who takes a great interest in the evidence for life after
death. Morse explains that this girl died and went to heaven, only to be
revived and brought back to life. Morse asked her what she had learned
from her visit to the beyond, and she considered the question carefully
before answering, "It's nice to be nice."

When I was a teenager in the 1970s, the magazines I read always had
lots of ads for posters, and one of the most popular of those posters
offered a meditation, in what I suspect was intended to be poetic prose,
called "Desiderata." Many people have come across it at some time or
another, at least its more famous lines:

You are a child of the universe, no less than the trees and the stars.
You have a right to be here.
And whether or not it is clear to you, no doubt the universe is unfolding as it
should.
Therefore be at peace with God, whatever you conceive Him to be.
And whatever your labors and aspirations, in the noisy confusion of life, keep
peace with your soul.
With all its sham, drudgery and broken dreams, it is still a beautiful world.

What I find particularly noteworthy about the popular response to this little document is the belief—perhaps still fairly common—that it is a piece of ancient wisdom, produced many centuries ago. Some of the posters identified it as "medieval" and claimed that it had been written by a monk; others dated it quite specifically as having been composed in 1692; still others combined the two, apparently considering the late seventeenth century part of the Middle Ages. (The 1692 date, it seems, arose because the piece was discovered some forty years ago by the rector of an Episcopal church in Baltimore, who typed it out on church stationery—stationery that prominently featured the founding date of the church: 1692. Photocopying and careless reading did the rest.)

In fact, "Desiderata" was written in 1927 by a man from Terre Haute, Indiana, named Max Ehrmann. Ehrmann was a lawyer who worked at various times as a deputy state's attorney and as a credit manager for his brother's manufacturing company—and these items from his résumé may be significant. His attempt to articulate a peaceable, serene prospectus for daily life, even or especially in the business world, suggests that his key problem was how to maintain a sanguine and mystical temperament in a corporate and bureaucratic environment:

> Enjoy your achievements as well as your plans.
> Keep interested in your own career, however humble; it is a real possession in the changing fortunes of time.
> Exercise caution in your business affairs; for the world is full of trickery.

"Desiderata" is a masterpiece of sorts because it so perfectly translates nineteenth-century American Romanticism into the terms of modern middle-class life—a process that may be said to have begun in 1836 when a student in Bronson Alcott's Temple School in Boston answered Alcott's inquiry about the mission of his soul by saying, "I think the mission of my soul is to sell oil." Max Ehrmann is the perfect apostle of that prescient boy's gospel.

But "Desiderata" is scarcely the final word on this subject. Ehrmann's descendents now populate American bestseller lists as the stars inhabit the skies. The current bumper crop of books celebrating the joys of amorphous and sanguine spirituality seems to find an especially appre-

ciative audience among people whose daily lives are spent in bureau-
cratized environments that, they feel, oppress their spirits. There are
so many of these books that even listing them is a challenge, especially
because they tend to proliferate like some uncontrollable malignancy
of publishing. Clearly it was not enough to have the 1993 bestseller
Chicken Soup for the Soul, because we now have reached *A Sixth Bowl
of Chicken Soup for the Soul*—these accompanied by *Chicken Soup for
the Woman's Soul* (the most popular one of them all, with over three
million copies in print), *Chicken Soup for the Soul at Work,* and *Chicken
Soup for the Golfer's Soul,* plus many others.

Apparently there are a lot of people out there who have no desire to
vary their menu, but if they ever do drain the soup bowl of life to the
dregs, they may join the millions who have thrilled to Betty Eadie's
account of her "journey through death and beyond," *Embraced by the
Light.* She and Melvin Morse and Raymond A. Moody—whose *Life after
Life* of 1981 has sold over fourteen million copies—dominate the enormous market in books that promise us that there is a sweet, pastoral
Beulah Land ahead of us: no waiting, these books all seem to say, no
day of judgment, just immediate admission to the place where everyone is nice. (If you wish to know more, please consult Raymond Moody's
Web site, <www.lifeafterlife.com>.)

One who consults these books, and the multitude of books like them,
will soon realize that their counsel and their message are somewhat
less than earth-shakingly original and profound. But that is precisely
the point. The popularity of "Desiderata," to return to my first example, arose in large part from its power to give expression to the hopeful
desires of many people that "the world is unfolding as it should," that
I am "a child of the universe," that, in short, "it's nice to be nice." But
that cannot be the whole story of its success or the success of the other
books that tap into this vaguely spiritual message of consolation. There
is a deeper reason for the American fascination with this kind of spirituality: our passion for having the validity of our desires confirmed by
witnesses from the distant past or beyond the grave.

This phenomenon can be seen most clearly in two immensely popular books that I take to be particularly salient examples of these cul-

tural trends: Neale Donald Walsch's *Conversations with God* (1995) and
Marianne Williamson's *A Return to Love* (1992). Each of these has produced its own sequels and spinoffs, as have all the books I have mentioned—Gutenberg's carcinoma striking again—but I want to focus
here on the originals. What they reveal to us is how deeply we Americans crave the echoing testimony of other times and places—as long
as they remain echoes and do not threaten to tell us anything unfamil-
iar or otherwise disagreeable. "Desiderata," in its guise as a monkish
meditation, brings us a confirmation from the past; its recent descendents, the books of Walsch and Williamson, offer us a still louder echo,
God's resounding endorsement of our every craving.

Walsch acquired what he calls "God's latest word on things" through
a highly traditional method: a kind of automatic writing in which Walsch
claims to have become the Deity's amanuensis (though one with the
power to scribble his own questions and responses). And what does
God reveal to Neale Donald Walsch? Well, for instance, that religious
institutions, persons of religious authority, and the Bible "are not
authoritative sources" for "truth about God." Instead, God says, here's
what we should do if we want to know about him: "Listen to your feel-
ings. Listen to your Highest Thoughts. Listen to your experience. Whenever any one of these differ from what you've been told by your teachers, or read in your book, forget the words."

This is certainly encouraging—not that I hadn't heard it already from
Timothy Leary, Abbie Hoffman, and the people who make those "Question Authority" bumper stickers. But a person with even the dimmest
spark of critical reflectiveness might be tempted to ask, "How can I tell
my Highest Thoughts from my lower, and presumably less worthy,
thoughts?"

This is a problem that Walsch's God doesn't quite know how to
address because he likes the sound of capitalized phrases like "Highest Thoughts" and "Who You Are" and so on, but he also is at pains,
repeatedly, to say that there is "no such thing" as right or wrong, better or worse. "There is only what serves you, and what does not." And
perhaps this is the key to understanding what our Highest Thoughts
are: they are the ones that are most perfectly self-serving.

Take our thoughts about money: at one point Walsch's God suggests that we need to "outgrow" a love of money, but when Walsch complains that he is financially strapped—"What is blocking me from realizing my full potential regarding money?" The Lord of the universe responds with almost gushing sympathy: "You carry around a feeling that money is bad." If only Walsch would stop feeling guilty, he could liberate himself to make and enjoy lots of money. Here's a counsel Walsch is quick to warm to: "I see I have a lot of work to do," he says with evident relish. Presumably, now that *Conversations with God* has been on the bestseller lists for several years, he has had ample opportunity to cultivate the requisite virtue.

The God of Marianne Williamson's *A Return to Love* bears striking similarities to the one Neale Donald Walsch hangs out with, which seems a confirmation of some sort—but a confirmation of what? In any case, Williamson's book is also based on a revelation given through automatic writing, though she was not the recipient. She is drawing on a hefty volume called *A Course in Miracles*, which came about in 1965 when Helen Schucman, a professor of medical psychology at Columbia University, heard a voice speaking to her that she came to believe was the voice of Jesus. Her colleague William Thetford served as amanuensis as the revelations poured forth; eventually the transcriptions made their way into print. (A comic moment occurs in some print and Internet versions of the story, when we are told that Jesus began by speaking these words to Dr. Schucman: "This is A Course In Miracles®. Please take notes." It makes one wonder who registered the trademark and where the royalties go.) But if Schucman and Thetford were the evangelists writing this new gospel, Marianne Williamson has turned out to be their apostle Paul, spreading the good news far beyond its original source.

Aside from dependence on automatic writing, or "scribing," another feature shared by Walsch and Williamson is their retention of much of the language of traditional Christianity, even down to the identification of God as a Trinity: Father, Son, and Holy Spirit. (It's Walsch who occasionally inserts references to God as Mother, while Williamson uses "He" and "Him" throughout.) A cynical reader might see both of these traits as attempts to borrow some external authority to buttress their claims and assertions—especially because the resemblance to Christian doctrine is merely verbal and never substantive. For instance, Walsch reinterprets Father as "knowing," Son as "experiencing," and Spirit as "being." Likewise, Williamson says that the Holy Spirit "has been given by God the job of . . . outsmarting our self-hatred. The Christ does not attack our ego; He transcends it." Thus she quotes *A Course in Miracles*, and remember, this is supposed to be Christ speaking: "Do not make the pathetic error of 'clinging to the old rugged cross.' The only message of the crucifixion is that you can overcome the cross. Until then you are free to crucify yourself as often as you choose. This is not the Gospel I intended to offer you." (In other words, "Forget that 'Take up your cross and follow me' stuff—I was misquoted.") Williamson again: "In the eyes of God we're all perfect," so our job is to recognize that. Evil is but an illusion.

Moreover, "the word Christ is a psychological term. . . . Christ refers to the common thread of divine love that is the core and essence of any human mind." A century and a half ago Ludwig Feuerbrach brought as his gravest charge against Christianity that it is the projection of our own desires—a claim that seems to be cheerfully accepted by both Walsch and Williamson, who are, when it suits them, pantheists who see God in all things, and therefore see God in us and as us. We like having a God who is a projection of our desires, because that God won't say anything we don't want to hear.

How do we account for the similarities between these two products of automatic writing? Did God speak to them after all? Or might it be more reasonable to consider the possibility that people socialized into the same American culture, with its pious and unquestionable commitment to liberal tolerance, its belief in the power of self-help, and its profoundly Romantic aesthetic sensibilities, would hear God saying the same things?

What is truly amazing about all this is that it never seems to have occurred to any of these people to question the validity of what they were hearing, or to notice that when other people in the past, or in other cultures, have claimed to hear God speaking he seems to have said very different things and to have exhibited a very different character. (The vision God granted to the fourteenth-century mystic Julian of Norwich began with an image of a crown of thorns from which blood flowed copiously. It is upon this image that her later understanding that "all shall be well, and all manner of things shall be well" is based. If Marianne Williamson had seen *that* I would have to take her claims more seriously.) I believe that I, in any case, would have been not only surprised but deeply disappointed if I heard God speaking and he told me nothing that I could not have found expressed more eloquently by Emerson and Thoreau, or for that matter by Dale Carnegie or Gail Sheehy. To come down from Mount Sinai with glowing countenance, only to have to tell the assembled masses, "I have heard God, and he is Norman Vincent Peale"—well, it's a fate I would not choose for myself.

How do we account for the tranquil composure, the utter lack of critical suspicion, with which Walsch and Williamson (and before them Helen Schucman) receive their remarkably unimaginative gospels? Sad to say, the answer appears obvious: they share the almost universal human susceptibility to flattery, and the God who speaks to them offers nothing but flattery. "I have nothing to tell you that you don't already know," he says. "You have understood yourself, your neighbors, and your social environment with admirable clarity. Your only problem is that you don't trust your own discernment. I can neither correct nor admonish you, but merely encourage you to follow your natural inclinations, which are infallible." Or, as Walsch's God puts it, "You all think very highly of yourself [*sic*], as rightly you should."

That's pretty much what these books are all about. Thus Iyanla Vanzant concludes the acknowledgments page of her popular *In the Meantime: Finding Yourself and the Love You Want* by writing, "And I would humbly like to acknowledge my Self for being willing to move through the fear, denial, confusion, and anger required to figure out why I had to write this book," and concludes the book itself by saying to her reader, "You, my dear, have become the light of the world—the loving light. I beseech you to do everything in your power to let your light shine." Having looked upon themselves with smitten wonderment, these authors turn to us and offer us the same celebratory gaze. (Thanks.)

All of our problems, on this account, are problems of perception; we do not see things clearly. Williamson tells this story: when she was working as a cocktail waitress, she was unhappy until she had the realization that "This isn't a bar, and I'm not a waitress. That's just an illusion. Every business is a front for a church, and I'm here to purify the thought forms, to minister to the children of God." (But could you bring me my martini first and purify the thought forms when you're on break?) Therefore it is not moral growth but visual or perceptual retraining that we need. And, *mirabile dictu*, what is obscured by our now-clouded sight is almost always our own virtue. Persons from the past who were, in their time, thought wise and discerning have supposed that people are blind to their own faults, but now God has appeared to Walsch and Williamson and Schucman to explain that just the opposite is true. It turns out that our moral excellence is what we habitually disregard.

Another way to put this point is to say that what these books most fundamentally reject is the notion that our wills may be twisted or bent. The God of these books never for a moment questions, or allows us to question, the validity of our desires; he merely offers superior means for realizing those desires. Thus his willingness to serve as Neale Donald Walsch's financial adviser. And Williamson's book, while it may seem at times to be more directive and to require more self-criticism— "God's plan works" and "Yours doesn't," she says at one point—in fact relies just as much as Walsch's on self-interest and self-congratulation. We choose God's plan because it's the one that will give us what we want. "We must face our own ugliness," says Williamson, but only to discover that it's either superficial or illusory: "The ego isn't a monster. It's just the idea of a monster." When we see more clearly, the bad idea disappears, to be replaced by the image of a "dashing prince." Looking back at her life, Williamson says, "there's one thing I'm very sure of: I would have done better if I had known how." (We do no evil, we just make "mistakes.")

Several years ago, when Woody Allen was asked to explain his affair with his wife's adopted daughter, he offered this verbal shrug: "The heart wants what it wants." This is an acute and consequential tautology, because it tells us that there is no power capable of interrogating, much less redirecting, the heart that wants—the heart that does nothing but want. The God of these books congratulates the heart for wanting and stifles the voice of mind or conscience that would offer dissent or even query. He accomplishes this stifling by proclaiming that he but echoes, that the universe but echoes, the heart's howl of appetite.

Am I, after all, a "child of the universe"? It's worth remembering that the phrase doesn't originate with Max Ehrmann. In Dickens's *Bleak House* the congenitally feckless Harold Skimpole, upon seeing the orphan Esther Summerson, cries out, "She is the child of the universe," only to have the more discerning John Jarndyce reply, "The universe makes rather an indifferent parent, I am afraid."

But in one sense an indifferent parent is precisely what we want: a God who neither instructs nor disciplines, who offers neither warning nor chastisement, but who smiles wryly at our peccadilloes and laughs warmly at our charming idiosyncrasies—not a Father in heaven but a Grandfather, as C. S. Lewis once said.

Yet this indifference has its dark and terrible side: without instruction or discipline or warning or counsel, we wander witlessly into a universe whose child we may be but that is populated by our siblings, people just like us—which is to say, people who ardently pursue goods that are incompatible with the aspirations of their neighbors, as Thomas Hobbes pointed out back in the Middle Ages (that is, circa 1650). The numbers of those who want to be the starting quarterback or the homecoming queen or the new executive VP far exceed the number of desirable roles and places, and they always will. And people whose greed and lust have been connived at by a celestial Parent prove, when faced with the inevitable obstacles to their aspirations, to be anything but "nice" and to be concerned with anything but "purifying the thought forms." Thus the constant threat of what Hobbes called "the war of every man against every man"—nothing "illusory" about that war—and thus the shameless irresponsibility of people who make and propagate a merely verbal Deity who strokes and consoles our desiring hearts, reserving his condemnation for those who would remind us, in the immortal words of the Rolling Stones, that "you can't always get what you want." If Mick Jagger can figure this out, may we not expect as much of God?

Postscript, October 2000: I have just received, thanks to Jody Bottum of *The Weekly Standard*—who evidently enjoys doing this sort of thing to me—a copy of Neale Donald Walsch's *Communion with God.* I cannot resist quoting this passage from the accompanying press release:

> Whereas the earlier books took the form of question and answer sessions in which God was the Master Teacher to Walsch's inquisitive pupil, in *Communion with God* the two now speak in a single voice. As this voice addresses matters of life and death, love and faith, the book's style and form demonstrate that Walsch has indeed achieved the communion with God towards which, through the course of all his previous works, he has steadily been moving. Closely examining the illusions that lead humans to self-blindness, division, and misery, Walsch and God show readers how they too can attain a communion with God, profoundly changing their own lives—and the entire world.

Suggested headline for the mergers and acquisitions page of the *New York Times:* PUTNAM PUBLISHING ANNOUNCES FOURTH PERSON OF GODHEAD. And of course all the academic theologians will have to revise their inquiries into the problem of evil: "Why does a good God allow evil, and why does his hypostasis Neale Donald Walsch let him get away with it?"

14

A VISIT
TO VANITY FAIR

NOT LONG AGO I WAS DRIVING in my car, listening to one of National Public Radio's news programs, when the host informed me that all Hollywood was abuzz over a legal dispute between two executives of the Walt Disney company. Finding the story of no immediate interest, I tuned out—but only mentally; I left the radio on that station. A few minutes later my attention was recalled to the report by the voice of a print journalist who was covering the Disney dispute. She was describing the outlines of the conflict and the excitement the case had generated, apparently not just in Hollywood but among the whole of this woman's acquaintance.

What had shaken me from whatever reverie I was in was the tense thrill in the journalist's voice as she described the events that had led Jeffrey Eisenberg to believe himself mistreated by Michael Eisner and then to seek legal redress. As she outlined the varying apportionments of blame and credit distributed by the cognoscenti she had consulted, her fascination was vividly evident—indeed I could have sworn that she was feeling nothing less than joy as she discoursed upon the case she had been assigned to cover.

In one sense I was experiencing something quite common: the bemusement we feel when in the presence of someone who finds absolutely compelling a subject, event, or person that prompts no curiosity whatever in us. When this happens, various reactions are possible. We may think, "What is wrong with you that you find this so fascinating?" Conversely, we may think, "What is wrong with me that the object of your passion leaves me so utterly cold?" (The experience grows more intense when we feel alienated from larger groups of people. Many American conservatives, including some famous ones, expressed this sense of befuddled dislocation when their fellow citizens exhibited blissful indifference to the moral turpitude of Bill Clinton.)

So there was nothing special or particularly unusual about this experience—but something about it stuck with me all the same. I kept thinking about that woman's voice and its palpable tone of excitement. And as I recalled the incident, my mind kept circling back around to one small fact: the magazine this journalist worked for was *Vanity Fair*.

Vanity Fair. It's a phrase with a curious and significant history. The magazine we see on shelves today is a recent one, founded in 1983 and put in the hands of an English editor named Tina Brown, whose success with it led to her being named the editor of the *New Yorker*, where she had markedly less gratifying results. But as many readers will know, the current *Vanity Fair* actually reconstitutes a slick and satirical American magazine that was founded by Condé Nast—who was in those days a person rather than a conglomerate—in 1914 and made quite a name for itself before succumbing to the Depression and being folded into *Vogue* in 1936. Digging a bit deeper, Nast's *Vanity Fair* was actually the third American magazine so named; the first was published from 1859 to 1863—it was perhaps not the most appropriate fare for a nation in the throes of civil war—while the second appears to have been a rather risqué number that flourished in the last decades of that century and continued intermittently under the same name until Nast bought the rights to it. Many readers, though perhaps not the same ones, will also identify the phrase with a venerable line of women's lingerie.

For the lingerie company the aptness of the phrase is clear: the women who buy their products are presumed not to think ill of vanity, and surely they wish to be fair. One resonance in this use of the phrase involves the item of furniture called a vanity, which typically contains items used to enhance one's appearance and is surmounted by a mirror into which one can gaze, musing: "Mirror, mirror on the wall, who's the fairest of them all?" A vanity is a place where one makes oneself the fairest of them all, or as close to it as one can get, and the appropriate lingerie can certainly aid in this project. Or so, I suppose, the namers of this company were thinking when they made their choice.

The magazine, however, in each of its avatars, has had something different in mind: Thackeray's famous novel of 1848. The book, too, was slick and satirical, with its famously telling subtitle, *A Novel without a Hero*. A reviewer in the May 1865 *Atlantic Monthly*—looking back on the novel's great success in the years since its first publication—gave remarkably clear expression to the reaction that almost every reader of the book has:

> There is not a person in the book who excites the reader's respect, and not one who fails to excite his interest. The morbid quickness of the author's perceptions of the selfish element, even in his few amiable characters, is a constant source of surprise. The novel not only has no hero, but implies the nonexistence of heroism. Yet the fascination of the book is indisputable.

Almost every critic of the novel has noted that while Thackeray follows the conventions of his time in seeing to it that virtue (such as it is) is rewarded and the nearly omnipresent vice is punished, he seems unwilling or unable to make his "few amiable characters" interesting or vivid, especially in comparison to his scheming villains. Amelia Sedley and William Dobbin are famously dull—what could you expect from someone called "Dobbin"?—while we find ourselves compelled by the wicked temerity and manipulativeness of the well-named Becky Sharp. Clearly Thackeray felt the same way and was indeed not only bored by, but highly suspicious of, apparent goodness: as he wrote in another novel, *The Newcomes*, "The wicked are wicked, no doubt, and they go astray and they fall, and they come by their deserts; but who can tell the mischief which the very virtuous do?"

That "no doubt" is a nice touch, explicitly stating conformity to the reigning mores while implicitly calling them into question: "the wicked are wicked, no doubt" in this case suggests a great deal of doubt. And something like this tone became characteristic of both of the magazines to take their name from Thackeray's book: a sardonic knowingness about the world, a propensity for the sly wink that communicates both a tolerance of what established society calls vice and a refusal to be taken by the appearance of virtue. The ultimate effect of this double-meaninged wink is of course to cancel out moral distinctions. The good are not so good as all that, and the wicked not so wicked—plus the wicked are ever so much more *interesting*.

One sees the same equivocation in the preface Thackeray wrote when he had completed the novel: "Yes, this is VANITY FAIR, not a moral place certainly; nor a merry one, though very noisy. . . . Some people consider Fairs immoral altogether, and eschew such, with their servants and families: very likely they are right." This "very likely" has the same force as "no doubt" in the previous quotation. "But persons who think otherwise, and are of a lazy, or a benevolent, or a sarcastic mood, may perhaps like to step in for half an hour, and look at the performances."

What distinguishes Thackeray—and, presumably, his readers— from the scrupulous persons who "eschew" fairs? Maybe our author is lazier than those morally vigilant folk. On the other hand, he may be more benevolent: what they would call proper vigilance could possibly be judgmental arrogance, pharisaical superiority. Or perhaps it's not a moral affair at all but rather a matter of temperament: some folks are naturally sarcastic, others more earnest. What we do not question is Thackeray's wish to distance himself from those unwilling to pass at least *some* time enjoying such amusements as the fair has to offer.

But who are these people anyway? In Thackeray's Victorian context they are primarily the Methodists and the Evangelicals, that dour party of soberly dressed recusants who opt out of the entertainments and circuses (the fairs) of their world—people indeed beyond the pale of Thackeray's imagination, being as unknown to Amelia Sedley as to Becky

Sharp, and unrepresented in his novel, though they wouldn't have read it even if they had been prominent in its pages. But the ancestors of the Methodists and Evangelicals were the dissenters of the seventeenth century. The greatest of the dissenters, by common consent, is John Bunyan, and in John Bunyan's greatest book, *The Pilgrim's Progress*, the pilgrim named Christian and his friend Faithful visit a place Bunyan calls Vanity Fair. And thereupon hangs the tale I am telling.

There is nothing sarcastic about Bunyan's portrayal of the fair. He is in deadly earnest in his belief that such a fair is a place of mortal danger to the Christian. This is one of the many elements in *The Pilgrim's Progress* that is not wholly (or even chiefly) allegorical. In a very important sense it is a direct realistic representation of the kind of fair, with booths of games and merchandise, known to every market town in England. Christian barely escapes the place with his life, while his dear companion Faithful suffers almost every kind of torture imaginable before being "burned . . . to ashes at the stake" and then "carried up through the clouds" in a great chariot, "the nearest way to the Celestial Gate." The powers that be in Vanity Fair—who are merely allegorically *named* portrayals of the very judges, magistrates, and civic leaders who persecuted Bunyan and cast him into jail for unlicensed preaching—are simply and thoroughly evil. The torments they visit upon Christian and his friend cannot be winked at or satirically reinterpreted, any more than the stubborn commitments of Christian and Faithful in the face of every incentive to recant.

How do Christian and Faithful run so far afoul of the rulers of Vanity Fair? The answer is simple: Christian and Faithful determine, and say, that *there is nothing of value to be bought there*. It is not their refusal of any particular opportunity for gaming or any particular piece of merchandise that gets them in trouble; that might annoy one or another merchant but would not anger the custodians of the whole structure. Rather, it is their claim that the whole fair is devoted to worthless merchandise and sham entertainment that earns them total condemnation; they are taken immediately into custody when to the question "What will ye buy?" they reply simply, "We buy the truth."

Perhaps more telling still, when the judge, Lord Hategood, instructs the jury at the end of Christian and Faithful's show trial, he takes pains to say that the accused have broken the laws of the town of Vanity not only, as one might expect him to say, "in word and deed" but also "in thought (which is not to be borne)." Even, or rather especially, silent and internal resistance cannot be tolerated at Vanity Fair.

I hope it will be evident that reading this history backward illuminates what is important about it: the move from moral earnestness to satirical knowingness. What Bunyan flees from in quite understandable fear, Thackeray treats with detached irony—though now the same irony interprets and judges his age's equivalents of Christian and Faithful: "The wicked are wicked, no doubt, and they go astray and they fall, and they come by their deserts; but who can tell the mischief which the very virtuous do?" The veneer of moral discernment remains, but it cannot disguise the underlying moral equivocation.

In today's Vanity Fair, vice has ceased to pay to virtue the customary tribute of hypocrisy. In Kierkegaard's terms, there has been a full retreat from, a complete abandonment of, the ethical sphere; the aesthetic alone remains. And the aesthetic realm judges the world by a single criterion: interestingness. To the aesthetic sensibility there is no virtue but to be interesting, no vice but to be dull. And thus the thrill in the voice of the reporter recounting the story of Eisner versus Eisenberg. That story is in no discernible way edifying, but then the category of the edifying seems inoperative in that reporter's intellectual world.

But what's wrong with something's being interesting? Perhaps more than we might think. In a great essay called "Genius and Apostle," W. H. Auden discusses the conclusion of *Don Quixote*, in which the knight casts off his chosen (fictional) identity and reclaims the one with which he was born: "I am no longer Don Quixote de la Mancha but Alonso Quijano, whose way of life made people call me 'the Good.'" For Auden, the book must end at this point because "the saint"—which Alonso Quijano is—"cannot be represented aesthetically." The Don Quixote whom we have come to know "is innocent of every sin but one; and that one sin he can put off only by ceasing to exist as a character in a book, for all such characters are condemned to it, namely, the sin of being at all times and under all circumstances interesting." When being interesting becomes a way of life, becomes the sole criterion of judgment, it's time to leave town while we still can, muttering beneath our breath the invaluable—but perilous—catechism for visitors to Vanity Fair:

Question: What do you buy?
Answer: We buy the truth.

POSTSCRIPT

LIVES
OF THE ESSAYISTS

MY TITLE IS THAT OF A BOOK sure to remain unwritten. Why does it sound
vaguely comical, unlike "Lives of the Poets," which sounds noble—
maybe Samuel Johnson's prose has something to do with that—or
"Lives of the Novelists," which sounds at least interesting and potentially scandalous? Or "Lives of the Painters," which carries the aroma
of heroic strife (Michelangelo) or Bohemian liberation (Picasso)? "Lives
of the Dentists" seems closer in spirit to "Lives of the Essayists," though
there is no reason to think that dentists and essayists experience less
excitement than poets, novelists, or painters.

Leaving dentists undefended for now, let us call to mind Montaigne,
in the midst of France's religious wars, hiding Protestants in his own
house to protect them from mobs of his fellow Catholics; or Charles
Lamb caring for his sister Mary after she had, in one of her periodic out-
bursts of dementia, murdered their mother; or Hazlitt, with his sexual
extravagances, his failed marriages, and his descent into near-insanity
prompted by his (unrequited) love for young Sarah Walker. A pretty
racy volume could be cobbled together from such events, and yet—
"Lives of the Essayists." It just won't do.

And to be honest, the examples I have cited are not the norm. Hazlitt
did indeed have a turbulent life, but Montaigne and Lamb usually

enjoyed, or endured, regularity and predictability, as have most of their colleagues in essaydom. Essayists tend to find interest in the insignificant, as E. B. White among others has noted, because little of significance happens to them. Or little of obvious significance, for one of the recurrent strategies of the essay is to proclaim, or gradually discover, the instability of our distinctions between the important and the trivial. For this very reason my favorite title for an essay is Phillip Lopate's "On Shaving a Beard"—or maybe Hazlitt's "On the Pleasure of Hating." Montaigne's and Bacon's essays often have more evidently philosophical titles, but as philosophy, after Descartes, transformed itself into a specialized and increasingly academic discipline, that kind of essay got crowded out. The last great practitioner of the philosophical essay in the old sense, I believe, is Hume (though some with lower standards than mine would acknowledge Bertrand Russell), but Hume could get away with it because he also wrote lengthy philosophical treatises in the properly authoritative manner. (Sadly, Hume had a condescending attitude toward even his own essays, which he wrote for women on the assumption that genuine philosophy would be more accessible to them.) Curiously, the analytic tradition in modern philosophy pursues some technical questions that sound like great topics for familiar essays: Bernard Williams once conducted a seminar on luck and ethics, which led to a book on the subject by Martha Nussbaum; J. L. Austin wrote a well-known paper called "Excuses." But make no mistake, those ain't essays.

If the essay is anything, it is the discourse of the inexpert. But in a society that produces ever greater numbers of experts, with an ever-increasing number of subjects in which such people claim expertise, the cultural gaps that the essayist is called upon to fill grow fewer and narrower. Still, there are a number of human concerns—mostly pertaining to what used to be called manners and morals—about which the essayist retains some plausible claim to having something valuable to say. For such favors essayists are partly indebted to the poets' abandonment of some of their time-honored haunts, for certain kinds of reflection that we now associate with the essay were at one time part of the province of poetry—the Horatian epistolary and satirical tradition, for instance. Many of Horace's poems would not be written as poems today; in the aftermath of the Romantic confinement of true poetry to the spheres of the lyrical and the meditative, they would have to be essays instead. After Pope, or rather after William Cowper (the style of whose letters is often nearly indistinguishable from that of his long discursive poems), the Horatian tradition displaces into essayistic prose, with only a few exceptions of note, the later poetry of W. H. Auden most prominent among them.

As even this territory suffers the encroachments of experts, essayists start to get nervous; fearing that sedentary existence will leave them nothing to write authoritatively about, they get out of the study and into the Real World. Joan Didion travels to El Salvador, John McPhee comes into the country of Alaska, Edward Hoagland communes not only with turtles but also with red wolves and black bears, and Annie Dillard visits Tinker Creek and encounters some Chinese writers. (Montaigne kept a famous travel journal, but did not intend it for public consumption.) Indeed, it isn't surprising when essayists modulate into travel or nature writers, because it often seems that no one writes mere essays when something more glamorous—and almost anything is more glamorous—beckons. Few writers nourish as their highest ambition the hope of becoming an essayist; it appears to be the sort of thing you settle for when other options have petered out.

I must admit that I know this temptation well. A few years ago I found myself traveling to Nigeria. It was my first trip to Africa, and because Nigeria isn't a tourist stop—especially the remote area in the center of the country where I was headed—visions of piquant and perhaps even semidangerous adventures (of the kind that, recounted in a suitably fragmented style, might be published in *Granta*) danced in my head. I purposed to keep my notebook and pen near at hand at all times. But on the Brussels-to-Lagos flight I began to realize that the event might mock my hopes. An hour from Lagos I heard this scene enacted three rows behind me:

Flight Attendant (male, 50, bald, not quite avuncular): May I help you?

Passenger (slim Nigerian businessman, maybe 35): I want some orange juice.

Attendant (who is taking up cups, not offering drinks): Coke and orange juice together will make you sick.

Passenger (in a loud voice): I will drink what I want! Who the hell are you to tell me what I should drink?

Attendant: (inarticulate surprised sounds)

Passenger (shouting): I demand an apology from you! I demand to speak to your superior! Who the hell are you to tell me what to drink? I will drink orange juice and Coke if I damn well want to drink orange juice and Coke!

Later, after the chief attendant spoke to both of them separately, there were muffled words of apparent reconciliation. The whole scene was genuinely disturbing, of course, but at the same time I felt that I was sitting through a one-act play written by college sophomores who had been given the task of adapting a V. S. Naipaul novel. A five-minute course in postcolonial anxiety.

Perhaps, I thought as I shuffled off the plane into the viscous air of Lagos, the airline provides this sort of display as a public service for first-time Western visitors to Africa. Perhaps the veterans paid no more attention to it than to the instructions at the beginning of the flight about the proper use of flotation devices.

Again and again during my stay in Nigeria I had this sense of being cut to fit the Procrustean bed of contemporary accounts of Third World travel. The most memorable moment of all came when I went with a group of Americans to the large central Nigerian city of Ilorin to look for somewhere to eat. In the basement of what was allegedly the only hotel in Ilorin we found a Chinese restaurant, of all things, run by a couple from Hong Kong. "Did you notice the satellite dish in the parking lot?" my host asked, in a Chinese-Nigerian accent. Indeed I had. "That belongs to me," he said with pride, and as we ate cashew chicken he wheeled out the TV and turned it on. The station he first found was showing *Bewitched.* Later he fiddled with his dish in hopes of picking up CNN, and eventually I was able to find out how the Orioles were doing.

That night, back in the little tin-roofed house where I was staying, I dutifully recorded the incident in my notebook. But even as I did I shook my head. Thirty years after the departure of the British colonial government, the story I had to tell was already an old one, with morals too obvious to draw. The homely life of the essayist was no more predictable than this, I thought, as I simmered until bedtime in Nigerian humidity and my own homesickness.

Still, I suppose it means something that in disparaging this kind of story I've managed to get mine told.

Montaigne suggests at several points in his *Essays* that he settled for his project of self-reflection and moral evaluation only because of his profound intellectual limitations: his terrible memory, his inability to pursue sequential and cumulative thought, his general mental slovenliness. He eventually came to believe that his belatedly accepted task was among the highest and best in which he could engage, but he did not come to it willingly; he was forced into it by what he felt to be a general ineptitude for other kinds of writing. Similarly, neither Lamb nor Hazlitt started writing essays with any degree of regular commitment until they were in their midthirties. And one wonders whether, like so many other successful essayists, Annie Dillard finally wrote a novel because she felt that this was the best way to prove that she is a Serious Writer. There is something at least potentially professional, even expert, about writing fiction; the essay is the sort of thing people do in their spare time, as can be seen in the titles of John Updike's hefty collections of his essays and reviews: *Picked-Up Pieces, Hugging the Shore, Odd Jobs.* According to these metaphors, essays are the potentially recyclable refuse of writing, the unskilled labor of literature. In the battered, leaky craft of the essay, one dare risk no more than a brief jaunt along a placid coastline, whereas in the mighty ocean liner of a novel one can presumably hazard even the roughest seas with confidence (or perhaps hubris—remember the *Titanic,* Mr. Updike).

Similarly, one of the blurbs on the back cover of Walker Percy's posthumously published collection of essays, *Signposts in a Strange Land,* says explicitly that the book will be valuable if and only if it stimulates interest in Percy's fiction. This seems like an odd choice for a blurb, since it might well scare off potential buyers who are *already* interested in Percy's fiction; but I was glad to be told, because otherwise I might have thought the book's contents valuable in their own right. One can find a similar condescension among academic literary scholars, whose work, especially if theoretical in intent or tone, represents itself as aspiring to a different and higher intellectual plane than the merely belletristic one occupied by the essay.

I find myself rehearsing such thoughts as I meditate on my own love for writing essays, on the satisfaction such work has always given me even as I have sometimes cast about for more expansive and culturally potent forms of writing. I am now just at the age at which Lamb and Hazlitt *became* essayists, as it were—an encouraging thought, because I can imagine no better fate than to become just such an animal, though I cannot hope to be so fine a specimen. But then I have always thought of the essay as a genre superior to those in which, as an academician, I have been trained to engage. In writing essays I at once do what I like and enter into a tradition that I feel unable to live up to, even though it may be found trivial by the greater part of the university's literary culture.

One of the great moments in Lamb's writing comes when, in the midst of an essay that has inexplicably and by a series of almost imperceptible movements changed its emotional course, he pauses and says: "I do not know how, upon a subject which I began treating half-seriously, I should have fallen upon a recital so eminently painful." That this confession was not at some later stage in Lamb's compositional process edited out, the evolution it describes smoothed over by the leveling hand of revision, strikes me as a perfect illustration of one of the distinguishing traits of the essay, its humble mutability of tone, its embrace of afterthoughts and further considerations. It often exhibits a palimpsestic character that no self-respecting genre would condone. But surely the world needs at least one literary genre that politely refrains from self-respect.[4]

---

4. I first came across that passage from Lamb in an essay by Phillip Lopate called "Whatever Happened to the Personal Essay?" which raises an incidental but interesting question: why do so many essayists write essays about essays? In some writers the tendency must be linked to the feeling that their chosen genre requires defense; but I think a more common reason is that the essayist has the opportunity that few have, to do one's work and talk about doing one's work *simultaneously*. When talk is one's job, then how can one tell the shop talk from the shop?

It seems to me that the loss, or refusal, of self-respect is one of the characteristic afflictions, or liberations, of middle age, and perhaps the essay is the great genre of the middle-aged. Of course many novels are about middle-aged people, but it seems that more often than not such characters are in various stages of rebellion against their time of life. Sometimes, as in Barbara Pym's books, those rebellions are so gentle and befuddled as scarcely to deserve the name—maybe "vague unease" would be more accurate than "rebellion." But the great essayists seem to be pretty comfortable with middle age, and perhaps even arrive there sooner than other people. Perhaps also (here is some wishful thinking) they tend to linger in what is for them a rather *gemütlich* territory and forestall by their very placidity the advent of geriatric anxieties.

My father—who is, among other things, a living compendium of old Southern adages—often reminds me that "if you can't run with the big dogs, you might as well go lie on the porch." It seems to me that essayists learn early on what many never learn at all: that the porch can provide a fine vantage point from which to observe the heroics, or the antics as the case may be, of the big dogs. And serious reflection comes so much more readily when one is protected from the heat of the sun and the cold of the pelting rain. Yes, a nice covered porch is the place for me—even if that decision merely further confirms what was already certain, that no future Dr. Johnson will find my biography worth writing. That does not mean, though, that I would be unwilling to conceal the occasional persecuted Protestant or to nurture a homicidal sibling. My life could use a little spice.